CHARMED LIFE

Tom Chalkley

Charles Cohen

Brennen Jensen

WOODHOLME
HOUSE
PUBLISHERS

Baltimore, Maryland

© 2000 Scranton Times t/a City Paper

All rights reserved. No part of this book may be reproduced or transmitted in any form or by any means, electronic or mechanical, including photocopying, recording, or by any information storage and retrieval system without written permission from the publisher.

Printed and bound in the United States of America.

1 2 3 4 5   09 08 07 06 05 04 03 02 01 00

Library of Congress Cataloging-in-Publication Data

Chalkley, Tom, 1955-
Charmed life / Tom Chalkley, Charles Cohen, Brennen Jensen.
    p. cm.
  Collection of columns entitled "Charmed life" from
Baltimore's City paper published in 1998 and 1999.
  ISBN 1-891521-09-8
  1. Baltimore (Md.)—Civilization—Anecdotes. 2. Baltimore (Md.)—Biography—Anecdotes. 3. Baltimore (Md.)—Social life and customs—20th century—Anecdotes. I. Cohen, Charles, 1962- II. Jensen, Brennen, 1963- III. City paper (Baltimore, Md.) IV. Title.
F189.BI5 C48 2000
975.2'6—dc21   00-040856

Woodholme House Publishers
131 Village Square I
Village of Cross Keys
Baltimore, Maryland 21210
Fax: (410) 532-9741
Orders: 1-800-488-0051
email: info@woodholmehouse.com

Book and cover design: Jason Lawrence
Backcover photograph: The authors under North Avenue bridge by Sam Holden
Cover art: "Bromo Seltzer Tower" by John Ellsberry

Charmed Dedications

To Ruth Quinn and Craig Hankin.
TOM CHALKLEY

To my father, Sidney Cohen, who inspired me with stories of old Baltimore; to my wife, Amy Lynwander, who put up with me while I set out to find stories of my own; to Sam Holden, who turned images into icons; and to Andy Markowitz, who helped me turn my ideas into articles.
CHARLES COHEN

To my father, Dean Jensen, who read to me nightly when I was a tyke, sparking my love of language. To my mother, Betty Jensen, who, 'round about the same time, dragged me to flea markets and antique shows, sparking my love of things old and odd. And to Winona Ryder. Maybe now she'll return my calls.
BRENNEN JENSEN

We'll always trade what we've got for what we had before
Everybody's a fool for something, I'm a fool for Baltimore
Tom Meltzer
from the song "Baltimore"
by Five Chinese Brothers

Contents

Introduction
ix

Charmed History
1

Charmed People
39

Charmed Places
87

Charmed Things
145

Photo Credits
184

Column Credits
185

About the Authors and Editor
186

Introduction

My *City Paper* colleague Heather Joslyn once observed of Baltimore that it is a city "comfortable with its eccentricities." I'd go her one better: Baltimore is a city that is exceedingly fond of its eccentricities, considers them an integral part of its civic identity, reveres authenticity over flash, looks upon its funky nooks and crannies with affection bordering on reverence. That's why John Waters is our favorite son, why Brooks and Cal are the lodestars in the Bird heavens, why Haussner's will always mean more to Baltimore than the Hard Rock Café. It's why we started "Charmed Life."

Like most good ideas, it was stolen. Well, *adapted*. Shortly after I became editor of *CP* in February 1996, Heather—who came to Baltimore from upstate New York via Knoxville, Tennessee—handed me a book called *Knoxville's Secret History*, a collection of Jack Neely's award-winning columns for that city's alternative newspaper, *Metro Pulse*. Neely's MO is emphasizing the "story" in "history," telling the often-obscure tales behind people and places in Knoxville's past; Heather thought something similar might be a good fit for us. I read and thoroughly enjoyed the book, thought, *What a good idea*, and filed it away in that part of the brain where good ideas go to die.

Fortunately, a year or so later two of *City Paper*'s contributing writers, Tom Chalkley and Charles Cohen—independent of each other, and, as far as I know, of Jack Neely—pitched me ideas for columns of local lore. Tom wanted to poke and prod into forgotten episodes of the city's history; Charles was mad for its quirky architecture (*There's this amazing water tower in Curtis Bay...*) and wanted to explore various intriguing edifices. I added to the mix staff writer Brennen Jensen, who shares with Tom and Charles a love of Baltimoreana and the uncanny ability to spot a potential story just by walking down the street. (Sometimes I imagine the three of them perambulating through town, their heads snapping to at the sight of a possible column subject, as if reacting to a sudden noise.) With three distinct perspectives at our disposable, we decided not to limit ourselves to the "secret history" but to open wide the column's borders—to take in overlooked treasures past and present, be they historical, architectural, cultural, or human.

"Charmed Life" (the name was Tom's) debuted on January 7, 1998; 60 efforts from its first two years are collected herein. Our hope, in both column and book, is to tap into the strong vein of feeling Baltimoreans have about Baltimore—not rosy nostalgia or boosterism or more-hon-than-thou clubbishness, but a sense of our city's unique personality, and of the delight we take in the odder angels of its nature. To the extent that we've succeeded, we are indebted to the folks at the Maryland Historical Society, the Baltimore Museum of Industry, the Enoch Pratt Free Library's invaluable Maryland Room, and other keepers of the Baltimore flame. Thanks also to Gregg Wilhelm at Woodholme House for his instant and unflagging enthusiasm for this project; to photographers Michelle Gienow, Sam Holden, and Jefferson Jackson Steele for giving "Charmed Life" a look all its own; to *CP* art director Joe MacLeod, whom I kept asking for help on this book and who kept delivering; and to all the folks, within *City Paper* and without, who have offered up ideas and encouragement. Most of all, thanks to the people who told us their stories so we could tell them to you.

Andy Markowitz
Editor, *City Paper*

Charmed History

French Connection

Every year around this time, chain restaurants, local bars, and theme-party hosts hitch a ride on the Mardi Gras bandwagon, but no one disputes that Fat Tuesday really belongs to New Orleans. Even Marylanders who make the bayou pilgrimage to get crazy and beg for beads are merely dabbling in someone else's culture. Had our forebears been a little more welcoming back in the mid-18th century, however, the Mambo King might have ruled on Charles Street as well as Bourbon Street. But the more than 900 Acadians who arrived in Maryland in the 1750s didn't stay long enough to establish a tradition of Ash Wednesday hangovers here.

The new arrivals were among some several thousand Acadians expelled from Nova Scotia because they refused to swear allegiance to Protestant Britain, which had gained control of the colony in 1713 and was concerned about the loyalty of its Catholic, French-speaking subjects. The Acadians had insisted on remaining neutral in ongoing disputes between France and Britain over Canadian territory.

After four decades of uneasy coexistence, thousands of Acadians were herded up in 1755 by Maj. Charles Lawrence, Nova Scotia's hard-line British governor, and sent packing. Their property and livestock were confiscated to pay their traveling expenses. Some were sent to England, others dispersed among its colonies to the south. The English hoped to assimilate the Acadians by breaking them up into small groups and immersing them in a Protestant, English-speaking society.

A large chunk of the exiles—913 people from the Nova Scotia settlements of Grand Pré and Pisiquid—landed in Annapolis in November 1755. Maryland and Pennsylvania, which had reputations for religious tolerance, "should have proved the most hospitable [of the English colonies] to the homeless French Neutrals," Carl A. Brasseaux writes in his book *The Founding of New Acadia*. But Maryland in the mid-1750s was not in so welcoming a mood: The colony faced a security threat from French settlements in the Ohio River Valley, on its western border.

By the time the Acadians landed—in overcrowded ships that were virtually barren of supplies—Marylanders had already been whipped into a Francophobic frenzy by the Annapolis-based *Maryland Gazette* newspaper, which characterized the Acadians as having a "proclivity for looting, homicide, arson, and rape." The colonial government wasn't keen on caring for the exiles; it passed a law requiring that Acadians work or be jailed, it restricted their travel, and it basically issued a shoot-to-kill order for anyone trying to make their way into the French territories to the west. Groups of Acadians were carted off to various Chesapeake settlements, including Baltimore.

Maryland's treatment of the exiles might seem cold-hearted today, but Gregory Wood, a Wheaton schoolteacher and author of the book *A Guide to the Acadians in Maryland in the 18th and 19th Century*, notes that in Colonial times, having 900 strangers show up at your doorstep must have been quite a shock.

"Imagine when they came in 1755," Wood says. "Annapolis only had 1,000 people. What if a population about the size of your town was out in the Severn River wanting to land? You can bet people were scared."

For years the Maryland Acadians languished, dying of pneumonia, smallpox, and malnutrition and receiving charity only from a few people. "Forced to make their own way," Brasseaux writes, many "grudgingly accepted low-paying and often degrading jobs offered by their reluctant hosts and gradually improved their lot, though never rising above poverty level." The Baltimore Acadians fared somewhat better than the rest, using their maritime experience to find work as sailors and longshoremen while their compatriots in Oxford, Snow Hill, and Port Tobacco toiled as plantation laborers.

Carl Lindahl, a University of Houston folklorist who has studied the medieval festival tradition, says that while he assumes the Acadians carried on their French carnival tradition when they lived in Canada, it would have been difficult for them to do so in the face of the hostility and deprivation they faced in Maryland.

"I don't know how well they had a chance to settle," he says. "I do know in recent history—although it's risky to make comparisons in history—when there was big trauma [such as the Civil War or World War II] they suspended Mardi Gras."

The Maryland Acadians continued to hope the French would eventually run the English out of Canada, but their hopes were dashed by the Seven Years' War. They turned their attention toward Louisiana, where other Acadians had begun settling in earnest in the 1760s. Maryland and neighboring states were more than happy to help their Acadians leave. Between 1766 and 1770, according to Brasseaux, some 90 percent of the Maryland and Pennsylvania Acadians took boats bound for Louisiana. There, settling back into French-speaking communities, they established what became Cajun culture (the name is a bastardization of "Acadian"), and eventually the Mardi Gras party-down tradition took root.

The Acadians who remained up here settled mostly around Charles and Lombard streets in an area that became known as Frenchtown, Wood says. They became merchants and seamen, and a few fought in the Revolutionary War. Some married into prominent families; some contributed to the local Catholic Church. But by the 1830s this Acadian presence had largely disappeared, and so had Frenchtown.

Charles Cohen
February 25, 1998

Blood Money

If you could take a time-machine trip back to late-1880s Baltimore, you might hear the ballad of John Thomas Ross and Emily Brown sung as you strolled the city's cobblestone streets. This macabre ditty recounts a brutal murder that was Baltimore's—if not the country's—only case of "burking."

The American Heritage Dictionary offers three definitions for the verb "burke," including "to suppress or extinguish quietly" and "to avoid; disregard." But it's the final definition that's relevant here: "To execute by suffocation so as to leave the body intact and suitable for dissection." We owe the term to one William Burke, an Irish-born grave robber who tired of digging up corpses—and started producing them instead. He's thought to have killed 32 people in Edinburgh, Scotland, in the 1820s, plying victims with liquor and then suffocating them. The warm corpses were trucked down to the local dissection room and turned into cold cash. (Anatomical study was a burgeoning field then and test subjects were bought on a cash-on-the-coffin basis.)

Baltimore's burkers were less subtle men, substituting bludgeoning and stabbing for strangulation, but their motivation was the same as that of their forebear. In 1886 they killed Emily Brown and sold her corpse to the University of Maryland School of Medicine for $15.

In contrast to its brutal end, life began pleasantly enough for Miss Brown. The daughter of an Easton hotelier, Brown was a talented seamstress who spent her early years in bourgeois comfort. But in the 1870s, middle-aged and unmarried, she drifted into Baltimore and developed a penchant for whiskey and opium. Begging became her avocation, a filthy flophouse on Pig Alley her address. (The ignobly named street ran smack in front of the site where Camden Yards sits today.) Another boarder at this tumble-down abode was Anderson Perry, a custodian at the nearby medical school.

"Uncle Perry," as he was sometimes called, concluded that beggar Brown was worth more dead than alive, and he convinced lowly associates John Thomas Ross and Albert Hawkins to do the dirty work. On December 10, 1886, the pair attacked Brown in her Pig Alley home—Ross beating her over the head with a brick, Hawkins knifing her in the chest for good measure. They stuffed her bloody body in a sack and wheelbarrowed it to the door of the med-school dissection room, where Perry awaited. The trio split their booty even-steven.

Had the men practiced proper burking, their fiendish plot might have gone undiscovered, but the medicos grew suspicious of the cadaver's wounds and alerted the police. The case unraveled quickly when the body was identified as Emily Brown's, and it was learned that Perry was her housemate. The custodian was hauled in and soon confessed all. But in the resulting legal wranglings, only Ross was implicated; he was hanged in 1887 in the yard of the city jail.

The cold-blooded, cash-driven crime shocked the city ("Burking in Baltimore" blared a front-page headline in *The Sun* on December 13, 1886). Every Baltimorean who went missing was assumed to have been burked. H.L. Mencken was a child at the time and recalls the burking hysteria in his autobiography *Happy Days*—writing (joshingly) that the University of Maryland med school "swarmed with medical students who never had enough cadavers to supply their hellish orgies." Mencken reports that the more fearful of his west-side neighbors wouldn't even walk past the school for fear of being yanked in and opened up. In actuality the Brown murder helped speed the enactment of laws that put the kibosh on the cash-for-cadavers trade. (Today a state anatomical board oversees corpse procurement; the bodies are obtained through voluntary donation or drawn from among the city's unclaimed dead.)

Baltimore's bumbled burking had one final odd twist. Some years after the crime, a fire swept through the med-school dissection room. As fate would have it, Anderson Perry's body was among the stiffs found within. (He had apparently died destitute and alone.) The more superstitious students came to blame the conflagration on Perry's ghost—incensed, perhaps, that his mortal remains had come to the same humble fate as poor Emily Brown's.

Brennen Jensen
March 18, 1998

Immigrant Song

In Ronald Zimmerman's South Baltimore real-estate office, the walls are lined with turn-of-the-century photos in heavy frames—babies in Victorian-era finery, a group of gents in front of a church. A huge portrait of a matriarchal woman watches over the room.

A visitor asks if the pictures are of Zimmerman's kin. He laughs and points to the old lady on the wall: "I have no idea who she is."

But he does know what she represents. The photos are heirlooms, artifacts given to him by customers who've heard about his quest—to see to it that the South Baltimore port of Locust Point, known best as a site of shipbuilding and commerce, is recognized for its place in America's melting-pot history.

Up until the mid-1950s, Locust Point was one of the country's largest intake points for immigrants, at times running second only to Ellis Island. But while the small island in New York Harbor is recognized as the historical nexus of American immigration and still makes news (New York and New Jersey battled all the way to the U.S. Supreme Court over which state owns it), the place once known as "the other Ellis Island" is sorely in need of attention. There isn't even so much as a roadside plaque to mark the spot where thousands of German, Polish, Czech, Russian, Bohemian, and Irish immigrants first set foot on U.S. soil, to settle in Baltimore or to embark on the B&O Railroad for points north, south, and west.

Suzanne Greene's *Baltimore: An Illustrated History* tells some of the stories. According to the book, a thousand Bohemians came through Locust Point in 1880; 1890 brought 4,000 Russians, mostly Jews. A 1938 article in *The Sun* put the number of immigrants that had come through Locust Point by that time at 1.5 million, with the peak traffic in 1907, when 60,000 new Americans arrived under the gaze of the statue of Maj. George Armistead at Fort McHenry rather than under the watch of Lady Liberty.

Unlike government-run Ellis Island, Baltimore's immigration center was created by free enterprise, as described in "Forgotten Doors, the Other Ports of Entry Into the U.S.," a 1988 article written by Dean Esslinger for the Philadelphia-based Balch Institute for Ethnic Studies.

According to Esslinger, the B&O Railroad forged an agreement with the North German Lloyd Line, establishing rail-to-sea links to Europe. The *Baltimore*, the first steamship to sail as part of the pact, arrived in 1868. Immigration through Locust Point leaped from a few thousand people a year to tens of thousands. Many of the immigrants went through rigorous inspections in the German port before boarding the ships, but those who didn't get processed before reaching Baltimore had to stand in line for hours at piers 8 and 9 at Locust Point.

Today all that's left of the dock area and waiting rooms in which immigrants arrived and were processed is an empty plot of land next to Fort McHenry and a box of unfulfilled plans in Rob Zimmerman's office closet.

Zimmerman, a fiery, rough-and-tumble man who calls people "boss," has been carrying on a largely solo crusade to open a museum marking Locust Point's role in the immigration wave, either on-site on ground now owned by CSX or on some state property next to Fort McHenry. He knows he's dreaming big, trying to memorialize a place that no longer exists. But in a town that's trying for all it's worth to paint itself as a tourist Mecca, Zimmerman believes it makes sense to have a place where visitors can scroll through immigration records in search of ancestors and gaze at photos of well-dressed hopefuls eager to make their play in the New World.

"I've been in the business for 36 years," he says, "and if this thing doesn't work, I don't belong in real estate."

Just a few years ago his plans seemed to be taking off. Zimmerman says the idea had the support of, among others, City Council member Martin O'Malley and the Baltimore Museum of Industry. In 1994 architects volunteered their time to draw up plans for the $5 million restoration of an old warehouse that was part of the Locust Point immigration complex, and the Ellis Island of Baltimore Foundation, a nonprofit organization formed by Zimmerman, received a $50,000 state grant for renovation of the building. The museum was set to open in 1996, but on the first day of that year, the warehouse was destroyed in a fire, and Zimmerman's dreams have been in limbo ever since.

"The museum at Ellis Island is very well done and it would be great to have something like that in Baltimore," says Ann Steele, deputy director of the Baltimore Museum of Industry. "But it's hard for the [museums] here in Baltimore and Maryland because there is a diminishing of funding."

There's no lack of cheerleading for Zimmerman's effort. "You can read the letters," he says, glancing down at a box of correspondence from supporters. "It's like they're crying, 'Please do it, Mr. Zimmerman.'" But, he says, "there's nobody that seems to want to step forward" with concrete financial support. "Somebody out there, someday, may pick this up.... That's where we're hanging," he says. "It's a possibility." But it's an increasingly remote one.

Zimmerman fears that as he struggles to erect his

monument, the city's role in immigration history is fading from the community's collective memory. He recalls presenting his proposal at a City Council meeting a few years ago and being greeted with disbelief that immigrants were processed in Baltimore. This chapter in Baltimore history, it seems, is fading into obscurity, like the identities of those pictured on Zimmerman's walls.

Charles Cohen
July 1, 1998

Postscript: Rob Zimmerman is still trying to get an immigration museum built at Locust Point.

Song of Ourselves

The music world has served our city some sour notes. Songwriters tend to paint Baltimore as a dirty, cruel, home-wrecking, and racist has-been. Remember how Randy "Short People" Newman's bleak ditty "Baltimore" twisted local knickers in a wad with its weary tale of drunks, hookers, and hard times? Bruce Springsteen's "Hungry Heart" advertised the town as a good place to abandon your family, while the country classic "The Streets of Baltimore" makes this seem a likely place to lose a wife. Even Bobby Dylan gets into the act. Does the strumming bard of Hibbing, Minnesota, describe the jaunty grace of a Baltimore clipper? The funky tackiness of Formstone? No. Dylan's "The Lonesome Death of Hattie Carroll" recounts a racist goon's fatal thrashing of a black Baltimore hotel employee. It's almost enough to make you burn your radio and move to Washington.

Fortunately, there's "Baltimore, Our Baltimore," the city's

official municipal anthem. This four-verse hymn extols a "beauteous city" founded by statesmen, enhanced by parks and gardens, and rife with brotherly love. This happy Baltimore is everything Randy Newman's hapless burg is not.

If you didn't know we had an official municipal anthem, you're not alone. Seems this lilting paean to all things charming about Charm City is fast fading into the sunset of distant memory.

It was back in 1916 that lyricist Folger McKinsey (a *Sun* columnist) and composer Emma Hemberger each won $250 in gold in a Municipal Song Contest sponsored by Mayor James Preston and judged by the director of the Peabody Conservatory of Music and other lofty muck-a-mucks. A small orchestra and a professional chorus (backed by 300 sonorous high school girls) gave the tune's debut performance on Washington's birthday that year.

And since then? Many longtime Baltimoreans I talked to grew up singing the song in school classrooms in the 1950s and '60s, but more recently its strains have vanished from the public ear. A clerk at Shubert Music House in Pikesville was mystified by a telephone request for the sheet music to "Baltimore, Our Baltimore"—until I sang her a snatch: "Baltimore, where Carroll flourished/And the fame of Calvert grew!"

"Oh, that!" she gushed. "I learned that in elementary school." Her singing was audible as she scurried off to check inventory. But the store didn't have the music, and the clerk couldn't recall getting a request for it in more than a decade.

At City Hall and its various offshoots, the song is an even wispier memory. The Mayor's Advisory Committee on Arts and Culture reported never using "Baltimore, Our Baltimore"; ditto for the Baltimore Office of Promotion. The person responsible for overseeing what's left of the city school system's music curriculum did not return phone calls. There was some recognition at the Baltimore Symphony Orchestra, which last performed the city's official song at Memorial Stadium during the 1969 World Series. (The BSO retooled it as a march.)

Transplanted Baltimorean that I am, the only place I've heard the song is on a 78-rpm record the now-defunct department store Hochschild Kohn and Co. released in 1921 (in celebration of its 24th anniversary). Given the limited amount of recording space of early records, only the first and third verse are performed, with baritone Hobart Smock singing the first verse solo. Smock is listed in the 1921 city directory as a Towson insurance salesman (according to a friend of mine who has enough time on his hands to check such things). The Manhattan Male Quartet backs Smock on the third verse. (Even accounting for the primitive recording technology, the four guys sound, well, like they downed a few Manhattans before stepping up to the mic.)

But even in this crude rendition, "Baltimore, Our Baltimore" emerges as a pretty song. Mayor Preston asked for something both "dignified" and "rousing," and the McKinsey/Hemberger creation seems worthy of the golden prize. It might be a little turgid for today's rhythm-oriented ears, but it's refreshing to hear a bit of Baltimore boosterism that doesn't rely on the dog-eared touchstones of contemporary civic pride (the Orioles, the Inner Harbor, crabs). The anthem honors the hoary names of yore: Carroll, Calvert, Key, Poe, and Lanier (as in Sydney Lanier, composer, poet, and erstwhile first flutist with the Peabody Orchestra). And for my money, "Baltimore, Our Baltimore" is miles better than the dippy state song, "Maryland, My Maryland," which has a recycled tune (from the Christmas carol "O Tannenbaum") and Confederate-sympathizing lyrics.

Though we don't have a bouncing ball you can follow, here's verse one of our official municipal anthem:

> Baltimore, where Carroll flourished,
> And the fame of Calvert grew!
> Here the old defenders conquered
> As their valiant swords they drew

Here the starry banner glistened
In the sunshine of the sea,
In that dawn of golden vision
That awoke the song of Key:
Here are hearts that beat forever
For the city we adore;
Here the love of men and brothers
Baltimore, our Baltimore!

Brennen Jensen
October 7, 1998

Awl-Mighty Mobs

*O*n November 3, Baltimoreans (well, about half of them anyway) will march to the polls to vote. Public schools will be closed and the evening's sitcoms will be interrupted as the results trickle in. All in all, it's likely to be a pretty quiet day. Electioneers won't besiege each other with brickbats and muskets. Voters won't be plunged into tubs of blood, stabbed in the sternum with shoemaker's awls, or kidnapped off the streets. Apathy, not anger, surrounds contemporary elections. What a difference 140 years make.

Baltimore's nickname "Mobtown" can be traced back to the street brawls and riots that greeted the start of the War of 1812. But the city really earned its menacing moniker in the 1850s, when politicking was a blood sport and election days had both a vote count and a body count. Chief agitator in this turbulent time was a secret fraternal faction that grew into a nasty, xenophobic political party. Billed as the American Party or the Supreme Order of the Star Spangled Banner, it was more commonly called the Know Nothing Party (from its followers' penchant for proclaiming "I know nothing!" when asked about their dastardly deeds). The party members hated immigrants (Germans and Irish in particular) and Catholics (who were often German or Irish). Organized locally into "clubs" with charming names such as the Plug Uglies, the Black Snakes, the Red Necks, and the Rip Raps, the Know Nothings took to terrorizing the populace on election day.

Their methods were crude but effective. While today we vote in secrecy, voters of that era brought their marked ballots to the polls with them. Know Nothing ballots were gaudily striped and easy to spot. When a voter approached carrying Know Nothing colors, he was greeted with backslaps and smiles. When a rival ballot was spied, thugs chanted "Meet him on the ice!" and pounced like feral dogs. Fists, paving stones, and knives were part of the arsenal, but the favorite weapon was the easy-to-conceal awl. Shoemakers used these pointed tools to punch holes in leather; the Know Nothings used them to punch holes in their rivals.

"Cooping" was another election-day gambit. Drunkards, vagrants, visiting farmers, shore-leave sailors, and other hapless souls were yanked off the street, corralled in dank cellars, and then dragged en masse to the polls and forced to vote the Know Nothing ticket—sometimes dozens of times. (This practice predates the Know Nothings—they simply copied it; a besotted and ill Edgar Allan Poe is said to have been "cooped" just days before his death in 1849.) One Know Nothing clan—the aptly named Blood Tubs—thrust opposing party members into buckets of blood trucked in from a slaughterhouse. Terrified and dripping with gore, these victimized voters discouraged others from opposing the Know Nothing ticket.

In 1854, the Know Nothings gained control of the City Council. Two years later, in a violent election wherein 10 people were killed and dozens wounded, Maryland was the only state to give its electoral votes to Know Nothing presidential candidate Millard Fillmore. Know Nothing Thomas Swann was elected mayor. (Though thuggery helped get him elected, Swann was an otherwise progressive politician who, among other notable deeds, birthed the city park system; under a different party affiliation he was later elected governor.) Election Day violence returned in 1858. Swann's mayoral opponent was strong-armed into voting against himself and conceded hours before polls even closed.

And where were the Baltimore police during all this? Understaffed and under a Know Nothing mayor's thumb, the force was as corrupt as it was ineffective. The rival Democratic Party had some rough-and-ready gangs of its own. (The Irish-dominated city wards were particularly well defended.) Many polling stations became armed camps bristling with musket barrels. A cannon was employed during a bloody skirmish around Belair Market in 1856.

But fighting fire with fire was not the answer to ending the outrage. State-level anti-corruption reform began in 1859. The Know Nothings reacted to the reform movement with a huge rally in Monument Square, chanting, "Come and vote, there is room for awl!" The speakers platform was decorated with a giant awl, and a blacksmith was on hand to make and distribute the threatening tools.

But by 1860, when the state plucked the city police force from the mayor's private purview, the Know Nothings were out of business. Just in time, of course, for Baltimore to be divided—and its streets bloodied—by the Civil War.

Brennen Jensen
October 28, 1998

A Dog's Life

After 20 years of breeding Chesapeake Bay retrievers, Janet Billups knows what she wants out of her dogs. She wants her dogs to be the toughest dogs on the block. She's not talking pit-bull tough. She's not talking ferocious. She's talking pickup-truck tough—the kind of dog that will outwork any breed.

"Just to see these dogs crack through the ice in a pond in December, that gives me goose bumps," Billups says, watching 4-year-old Clipper on a run. That type of act—plunging into icy waters—is what the Chesapeake Bay retriever has been nurtured for since its origins nearly 200 years ago.

The tale of this fine hunting dog—the best waterfowl-hunting canine there is, some say—begins in Sparrows Point, or so the story goes. No, there were no Chesapeake Bay retrievers frolicking in the salt marshes when the first settlers arrived in Baltimore. The breed owes its birth to a seafaring accident.

Legend has it that the retriever bloodline goes back to two Newfoundland puppies that were rescued from a boat off the Maryland coast in 1807. Of course, legend also has it that the retriever is the product of a mating between a dog and an otter, but in the case of the shipwreck story, there's some corroboration in the form of an 1845 letter penned by prominent Baltimorean George Law.

Law—whose account is cited in numerous newspaper articles about the breed as well as in Janet Horn's book *The New Complete Chesapeake Bay Retriever*—was on board his uncles' ship, the *Canton*, in 1807 when it came across a sinking English brig. The *Canton* rescued the crew as well as the two pups, which were dubbed Canton and Sailor. Law purchased the pups and gave both away: Canton, a black female, to one James Stewart of Sparrows Point and Sailor, a dingy-red male, to another man, who in turn traded the dog to Maryland Gov. Edward Lloyd, a denizen of the Eastern Shore.

Sailor and Canton were bred separately, one on the Shore and the other in the Sparrows Point area. Both were bred with spaniels and hounds to produce hunters prosaically called the Chesapeake dog. The Chesapeake's swimming and fetching instincts were passed on from litter to litter, according to Horn.

Horn, in an interview, says Canton's descendants took root in the Gunpowder River area, which was known for duck hunting. The author says the Carrolls Island Kennel, one of the first duck-hunting clubs in the state, became a major breeder of Chesapeake Bay retrievers. Little is known about Sailor's progeny, but throughout the 19th century his descendants flourished on the Eastern Shore as Canton's did on the western side of the bay. Both lineages attracted many fans.

In 1877, the products of those two lines were compared for the first time, at the Poultry and Fanciers Association Show at the Maryland Institute in Baltimore. The breeders discovered they had produced practically the same dog, independent of each other, on opposite sides of the bay. The dogs had two coats of fur (for insulation in the cold water), a powerful fetching instinct, and an inexhaustible love of swimming. In 1890, the Chesapeake Bay Dog Club formally recognized the dogs as a distinct breed—the first American-bred sporting dog. (It wasn't until the 1930s that they were named Chesapeake Bay retrievers, a designation that allowed them to participate in hunting trials that had been reserved for Labrador retrievers.)

Most of the early records on Chesapeake Bay retriever breeding are gone. The Carrolls Island Club is long defunct, and the building in Marshy Point (a peninsula that juts into the bay north of Baltimore) where its records were kept burned down in the early 1900s.

But Harry Weiskittel, who owns property that includes Marshy Point, has hunting log books dating back to 1854 that make reference to the retrievers. And there are several tombstones for late canines on his property.

Weiskittel recalls taking out hunting parties with Labradors, whom he'd watch dashing in the cold water to fetch ducks. Then he would proudly watch his Chesapeakes work, sometimes diving four feet down in the water to get a wounded duck. Eventually the other working dogs would get too cold and quit, but his dogs couldn't get enough of the water.

"I've never seen a Chesapeake quit," he says. "They are tough, greasy-coated dogs."

But these days, Chesapeakes are not just about working. While the early breeders of Canton, Sailor, and their progeny were producing strong, tireless hunters and collectors, they also managed to produce good-natured companions. Which is just fine with Janet Billups, whose favorite moments with her dogs involve running.

"People like to jog alone," she says. "With me, you're enjoying the solitude, but you have your friend with you."

Charles Cohen
December 23, 1998

On the Waterfront

The dilapidated brick shell of a circa-1840s warehouse looms impressively over Chase's Wharf, at the western end of Thames Street. Somewhere on this piece of Fells Point waterfront is the site of the nation's first black-owned marine railway and shipyard, established in 1868 after a surge of racial strife and labor strikes.

It was here that Isaac Myers established the Chesapeake Marine Railway and Dry Dock Company and launched his career as an African-American labor leader—history the

Baltimore-based Living Classrooms Foundation is marking with the $9.1 million Frederick Douglass/Isaac Myers Maritime Park at the Chase's Wharf site.

The park—which will be part of the National Historic Seaport, an alliance of Baltimore waterfront attractions—will include a working shipyard, with students restoring historic vessels, in keeping with Living Classrooms' nationally recognized mission of providing maritime-oriented education and job-training programs for primarily at-risk youth.

"It's not going to be an exhibit space where all the exhibits are behind Plexiglas," says John Kellett, director of the National Historic Seaport for the Living Classrooms. "There will be a working rail that will replicate the country's first black maritime railway."

While Douglass' contributions as an abolitionist, orator, and statesman are widely taught and celebrated, the formation of the Chesapeake Marine Railway—a watershed in post-Civil War black history—and Isaac Myers' subsequent work as a national labor leader remain largely unknown.

The company grew out of the disenfranchisement of blacks who had established a niche in the maritime trades as ship caulkers and longshoremen in the years leading up to the Civil War. "In 1858, white jealousy of black competition in the shipyards reached such a pitch that riots were instigated against black workers," according to a 1971 *Maryland Historical Magazine* article. African-American workers' troubles increased as European immigration increased, providing greater competition for the well-paying jobs. African-American caulkers embarked on a strike that erupted into violence.

In 1868, amid the labor strife and the increased competition for jobs, Myers and 15 others organized a cooperative to create the new company. Up until the Civil War, Baltimore had the largest population of free blacks in the nation; Myers and his partners tapped into the African-American middle class and their churches to support their business venture.

Joseph Reid, a Living Classrooms board member and co-chair of the maritime-park project, says the significance of creating a black-owned company through stock offerings cannot be overstated. "Race became a dominant factor that drove a lot of blacks out, and that was the impetus for Myers to create the shipyard," Reid says. Chesapeake Marine Railway further broke racial ground by employing blacks and whites side by side.

Lease problems forced the company to close in 1878, but by that time Myers had risen to national prominence, founding the Colored Caulkers' Trade Union Society and working with prominent African-American leaders to establish the Colored National Labor Union, on whose board Douglass sat.

To local historian Vincent Leggett, Myers' story isn't just history—it's a blueprint on how to reconnect the African-American community with its maritime heritage and steer it toward environmental activism.

For almost two decades, Leggett, a local historian and former president of the Anne Arundel County School Board, has driven the Maryland shoreline, recording oral histories, collecting artifacts, and piecing together the story of Maryland's black watermen. The role of blacks in Maryland's maritime history has received little attention, a knowledge gap Leggett links to the limited minority involvement in environmental causes. Many African-Americans, he says, "look at the Chesapeake Bay as a playground for the rich."

Leggett is trying to help fill that gap by establishing the Blacks on the Chesapeake Foundation, which is dedicated to raising awareness of African-American maritime history and rallying the black community to get involved in the environment. It's his mission to show that African-Americans have a cultural stake in protecting the environment that goes beyond simple civic duty. In Myers' ability to pull together community resources and reach out to the black middle class, Leggett sees a model for his own grass-roots efforts. His successes so far have included organizing the Clay Street

Development Corporation in a small African-American community on College Creek just outside Annapolis. By spotlighting the locals' heritage, Leggett says he encouraged them to clean up their shoreline.

Leggett says the African-American watermen he encounters on his travels are often suspicious of inquisitive strangers, smelling speculators out for waterfront land. But Leggett says the stories flow when the watermen realize it's history, not property, he finds valuable.

"We have found a way to bring dignity and pride to a community contribution that has not been present in that fashion," Leggett says. "Now people are calling me saying, 'Look, my mother was an oyster shucker' or 'My uncle worked on the water.' Before that people thought it was not significant, or just commonplace."

Charles Cohen
February 24, 1999

Postscript: Fund-raising and construction of the Frederick Douglass/Isaac Meyers Maritime Park continue apace. The park is scheduled to open in the spring of 2002.

Mobtown Motors

In local lore, 1904 is a date that will live in infamy as the year much of downtown Baltimore burned to the ground. But in terms of lasting impact, another event that year was far more important. In 1904, the state of Maryland enacted its first laws governing the ownership and operation of automobiles.

In bureaucratic terms, early motorists had it easy. Today

we face confusion and interminable lines at the Motor Vehicle Administration; our Maryland forebears simply mailed off a brief application and $1 to get their combination registration and driver's license (no parallel parking under the watchful eye of a grim-faced tester). Drivers were even instructed to make their own license plates. The Baltimore speed limit was set at a neck-snapping 6 miles per hour (though you could punch it up to 10 mph on country roads).

A grand total of 654 horseless carriages were registered in Maryland in 1904. Eighty were Oldsmobiles, but more than 70 other car makers were represented on state registration forms, including such long-lost names as Pungs-Finch, Panhard, and Peerless. (Three plucky motorists described their cars as "homemade.") Detroit had yet to get a lock on the industry, and cars were cobbled together everywhere—including Baltimore, home to a half-dozen early automakers.

A squat brick building that still stands in the first block of East Wells Street in South Baltimore was home to the Sinclair-Scott company. Sinclair-Scott's most famous invention was a mechanized pea huller, but it also built cars. In 1902 the firm started making auto parts under contract for other manufacturers; when one of its clients went bankrupt in 1904, Sinclair-Scott was left holding a pile of auto components and decided to put together a car of its own.

Sinclair-Scott's four-wheeled creation was called the Maryland, its name written in script across the radiator. It was a sturdy, painstakingly assembled, and well-engineered machine (Sinclair-Scott pioneered the overhead-cam engine) available in sports, standard touring, and deluxe models. The vehicle's 28-horsepower, four-cylinder engine could send it careering along at several times the legal speed limit. Henry Ford was reportedly so impressed with the Marylands he saw at an early Baltimore auto show that he asked Sinclair-Scott to merge with him. But the Maryland's makers looked down their noses at Ford's then-burgeoning mass-production methods and wheels-for-all mind-set. The Baltimore company's mostly handmade cars were works of art, and the lowest-priced model cost about $2,750 (a sum that at the time could get you a three-bedroom rowhouse). This princely price tag proved the Maryland's undoing—fewer than 400 of the cars ever rolled onto the street. By 1910, Sinclair-Scott returned full-time to the production of peapod machinery and canning equipment.

A number of other Baltimore car makers came and went during the auto's heady early days. There was the steam-powered Crouch (1900), the Lord Baltimore truck (1913-1915), and the Steinmetz electric (1920-1927). After the Maryland, the most successful Baltimore car probably rolled out of Carl Spoerer's Sons Company's Pigtown plant. Like many early automakers, the Spoerers began as buggy builders. They made their first car in 1907, and soon offered everything from a roadster to a limousine. Spoerer's machines were big and brawny, popular with everyone from racers to the Baltimore City Fire Department (which once used Spoerer fire trucks). In 1909, a Spoerer placed seventh out of 40 cars competing in the Munsey Reliability Run, a Washington-to-Boston round-trip race sponsored by *Baltimore News* owner Frank Munsey. (Something called an Elmore came in first; a Maryland finished 17th.)

But like the Maryland, the Spoerer's custom-built motorcars cost a small fortune (in this case, $2,000 to $4,000). By 1915, Ford's mass-produced Model T (which debuted in 1909) could be driven off the car dealer's lot for less than $400. Cars stopped being novelties for the rich, and Detroit became the Motor City. It's unlikely any Marylands or Spoerers even exist anymore. A member of the Antique Automobile Club of America (AACA) informed me by e-mail that there was "no record that either one of these cars has been shown in the AACA or been on tours." About all we have left to remind of us of Baltimore's early auto days is bumper-to-bumper traffic. When the misnomered "rush hour" is on, that old speed limit of 6 mph still seems to hold true.

Brennen Jensen
March 3, 1999

Green Acres

When my wife and I bought a house in Northeast Baltimore in 1993, it came with a sheaf of papers documenting the property's history. The oldest item is a 1918 plat, or property map, which shows our neighborhood ("Arcadia, the Land of Ideal Conditions") as a sort of honeycomb of rectangular lots. Our own little rectangle, on the eastern edge of the development, overlooks the Most Holy Redeemer Cemetery at Belair and Moravia roads.

According to a fellow Arcadian, Eric Holcomb, both our neighborhood and the cemetery used to be truck farms—agricultural tracts devoted to vegetables, fruit, and dairy goods. For the past two years, as Northeast Baltimore's quasi-official historian, Holcomb has been assembling documents and photographs into a panoramic jigsaw puzzle depicting life along the old corridors of Hillen, Harford, and Belair roads for a history he hopes to have published by Christmas.

One key to the puzzle is an 1877 atlas of Baltimore County that shows property lines and landowners' names. By cross-referencing the map with an 1882 *Maryland Directory*, Holcomb has sorted out which areas were devoted to farming, which to manufacturing, which to trade, and so on. Arcadia, for example, was carved from the Eutaw farm, which in 1877 belonged to one William Halls. The neighboring farm of Thomas Burgan became, in 1880, the Most Holy Redeemer Cemetery. Looking at the graveyard's green slopes, it's easy to imagine that cows once grazed on the land. It's harder to mentally erase the densely settled neighborhood of Gardenville, farther up Belair Road, but both sides of the old turnpike were once farmland, with a few shops and taverns lining the main drag.

Holcomb's analysis of local occupations—based on the 1882 directory—offers a glimpse of what 19th-century Gardenville (population 500) was like: Ninety household heads were farmers, seven were butchers, four were blacksmiths. Gardenville also included three brewers, three carpenters, and two each of druggists, dairy vendors, grocers, general merchants, and justices of the peace. All other occupations on the list claimed one resident each.

Physical remnants of the old farming community can still be found—notably the family grave plots spared by developers. On Furley Avenue, the tiny, well-kept Gontrum family cemetery suggests that the east side of Gardenville was a German settlement. Christian Gontrum (1792-1845) and his wife, Anna, immigrants from Hessen-Darmstadt, Germany, were the first of many Gontrums buried there, along with various Koenigs, Karchers, and Kienzles. Some of their stones are inscribed in German. Another small grave plot, wedged between commercial buildings on the west side of Belair Road near Parkwood Avenue, has stones with the names Burgan, Frankton, Wright, and Harryman. The site corresponds to a tract labeled "Mrs L Burgan" on Holcomb's 1877 map.

A few blocks north, at the intersection of Forrester and Oaklyn avenues, surrounded by tidy bungalows, is my favorite Baltimore cemetery. This was the burial ground of the Biddison family, which acquired 21 acres there sometime before 1812. The oldest legible gravestone is dated 1818. The plot shelters at least three generations of Biddisons, as well as folks named Forrester, Dietrich, McCauley, Henkel, Hollingsworth, and Hoey.

Why do these family graveyards contain such a variety of names? "All these families were interrelated," Holcomb says. "They all married each other."

What's obscured by surrounding development is that the Biddison cemetery is set on top of a gently sloping hill. Once, it may have commanded quite a view of the countryside.

Near the Biddison plot, on Frankford Avenue, stands the Andrew Chapel United Methodist Church, built in 1904 on land donated by the patriarchs of the Gontrum and Biddison families. The congregation had begun in 1853 as a breakaway from the Gatch Methodist Church on Belair Road; the flock parted over the issue of slavery, with the Andrew Chapel members taking a pro-Southern stand. The chapel's stained-glass windows are inscribed with some of the same names—Forrester, Burgan, Kauffmann, Otto—that crop up on the 1877 map, in the local graveyards, and on the street signs of neighborhoods that replaced the family farms. Stand at the corner of Belair and Frankford, and you can picture the little church as it must have looked on a rural roadside 95 years ago.

Tom Chalkley
May 12, 1999

Full of Beans

When Louis Pfefferkorn talks about his grandfather delivering fresh-roasted coffee by horse and wagon from Camden Street into the hinterlands of Ellicott City, it may sound like he's talking about the industry's good old days. But he's really describing the precursor to today's modern coffee-service industry.

"They would have regular routes," the 74-year-old head of South Baltimore-based Pfefferkorn's Coffee Inc. says of his namesake grandfather's horse-driven business—just like today's microroasters traversing the region in their vans. "They would call on people and these people would expect to see them. People today, they want UPS to deliver things. They order from the Internet. It [was] not too much different from that."

Indeed, by 1900, when the Pfefferkorn family decided to get out of the grocery business and concentrate exclusively on selling coffee and tea, the industry was entering the modern era—and the golden age of Baltimore's coffee business, when delivering the aromatic beans reeked of high-seas adventure, was fading.

Today, there are virtually no remnants of a trade that for a century and a half was part of the lifeblood of Baltimore's waterfront economy, when sailing ships laden with coffee beans from Brazil crowded the harbor. The ships and the men who sailed them are long gone; the few remaining records are like artifacts from a lost civilization.

"It's almost incredible that no complete and authoritative account of Baltimore's coffee trade with South America has been written," *The Sun*'s Ralph J. Robinson wrote in a 1951 article about a Maryland Historical Society exhibit, "The Coffee Trade of Baltimore." "Surely there is a need for such a volume and the field is fallow."

Baltimore's rise and fall as one of the nation's coffee capitals coincides with its history as a major sailing town with a reputation for shipbuilding and seamanship. In 1851, according to a brochure from the 1951 exhibit, no U.S. port, not even New York, was bringing in more of the magic bean. In the years following the Civil War, as much as 38 percent of the nation's coffee landed here.

The city's earliest forays into the coffee trade predate the American Revolution. As the most inland port on the Chesapeake Bay, Baltimore had great connections to mills deep in farm country that produced flour and grain for export; among the many products that arrived in return were small amounts of coffee from the West Indies.

In the early 19th century, with trade routes to the Caribbean well established, Baltimore and Fells Point merchants turned their attention to Brazil. Ships would venture down to Rio de Janeiro filled with flour bought from mills in Ellicott City and Ilchester and return with cargo holds full of coffee. But trading during these times was risky. Vessels could take months making the trip, and becoming lost at sea was a real danger. Merchants and residents would await the flying of a ship's flags from Federal Hill—a signal that the boat had been spotted rounding Bodkin Point (just north of Gibson Island) and its crew and cargo were home.

The story of the *Peggy*, recounted by Geoffrey M. Footner in his book *Tidewater Triumph: The Development and Worldwide Success of the Chesapeake Bay Pilot Schooner*, gives some insight into the dangers of the trade. On a voyage through the West Indies in 1794, the *Peggy* was twice captured by privateers and robbed. The captain had kept enough hidden from the thieves to purchase a cargo of coffee at a safe port to take back to the States, but on the way back he was knocked overboard by a boom, and died. Before the poor *Peggy* could make it back to the States, it was captured again, by privateers loyal to Britain. The ship was escorted to Bermuda and again relieved of its cargo before being released to return to Fells Point.

Such perils notwithstanding, Baltimore was becoming a dominant player in the coffee business, and remained so until the Civil War brought the trade to a virtual halt. Edward P. Duffy, *The Sun*'s marine reporter in the 1920s, wrote in a 1924 article about the Rebel capture of the Rio-bound *Empress Theresa* in 1864. The southerners torched the Baltimore clipper as its captain stood by on a Confederate warship.

With the war's end the following year, however, the port returned to even higher coffee-fueled heights. With commerce resuming unhampered, Baltimore merchants commissioned the building of special coffee boats called "barks" or "barkentines," later known as "coffee clippers" (although they were not built in the style of the famous Baltimore clippers). Bustling coffee warehouses sprouted on Brown's Wharf and Belt's Wharf in Fells Point. From 1869 to 1885, Baltimore's "coffee fleet," as it was known, was bringing in between 18 and 38 percent of coffee imported to the United States, mostly from Brazil. One sailing ship, the *Josephine*, made the trip from Rio de Janeiro in 22 days in 1893, setting a coffee-fleet record.

But as the 19th century drew to a close and "steam superseded sail," more and more of the coffee trade was concentrated in New York, according to the Maryland Historical Society exhibit brochure. Duffy—who interviewed surviving coffee captains in the '20s and celebrated their ships as reputedly "the cleanest and daintiest merchant craft afloat"—lamented in 1924 that "by force of change in the carriers of commerce, some were sold and others abandoned their high estate to become [carriers] of coal, lumber, and bulk cargoes.... Not one is afloat today."

These days, Louis Pfefferkorn, while using beans from around the world, gets most of his coffee delivered by truck. The beans are now mainly shipped to ports other than

Baltimore. But every now and then a container will come in by boat, arriving at the Dundalk docks.

Charles Cohen
August 18, 1999

Oil and Water

You've got to wonder about what we euphemistically call the "historical record." What gets included? What gets tossed into obscurity? Historians, especially the record keepers of yore, seem fixated on social standing and success as gauges of historical worth; sometimes they pass over the wilder characters, failing to capture the flavor, the soul of the times.

I've come across this soul deficiency over and over again as I roam from one obscure Baltimore historical tidbit to the next. My most recent encounter was with the story of oil refineries in Baltimore, a subject I honestly never thought about until I stumbled upon some articles in the Baltimore Museum of Industry's archive (and probably never would have thought about if I hadn't).

In this one pocket of Baltimore history, I found yet another mysterious character: a Frenchman known only as "Ponsi," who was the first person to sell a gasoline product in Baltimore. It happened in 1878. That's basically all the record shows.

I also came across the story of Sylvia Hunt, single mother of five and a refinery owner. Hunt stood up to John D. Rockefeller, who made his fortune in the late 19th century by monopolizing the oil business. Her dramatic story was rediscovered and pieced together more than a century later by David Heller, a former volunteer at the Museum of Industry, who saw brief mentions of Hunt in articles on other people and sensed there was something more to her story.

"She was a kind of individual who wanted to be in control of her own fate and couldn't stand someone else taking her livelihood," he says.

In the mid-1800s, refining was a dirty, chaotic business marked by blind experimentation and a desperate struggle to keep up with the technological changes of the Industrial Revolution. Extracting oil from coal was the trend, and refineries that did so cropped up in Baltimore, mostly on the Canton waterfront. These early structures were nothing like what we now think of as refineries, labyrinths of pipe and steel massed around highway interchanges—they were more like large shacks outfitted with primitive stills. Picture the Vermont maple-syrup industry plopped down in the lagoons at the base of smokestack Baltimore—except these refiners weren't sucking sweet syrup from trees, but trying to distill the juice from petrified coal to produce fuel for lamps.

Of course, this was decades before folks knew about toxic waste or cared about pollution; the refiners simply let the waste from their operations spill into ponds and wetlands. This is where we find the elusive Ponsi—down in the muck collecting industrial waste. According to records in the Museum of Industry archives, the intrepid Frenchman actually built a dam in ponds around Canton to collect the runoff from the coal refineries—a substance called "naphtha," which would become the raw material for gasoline. Ponsi would process the runoff at his own facility, also believed to have been located in Canton, and sell the results to Baltimore City to be burned in street lamps.

Heller—a chemist by trade who says he studies the early days of the oil industry "just for the fun of it"—notes that refining at the time was hardly an exact science. Coal processors wanted to produce heavier oils that could burn without exploding. But the refineries didn't always properly filter out the more volatile components, Heller says, and it wasn't uncommon for household lamps to explode or for refineries to catch fire. (In 1872, fear of fire prompted Baltimore residents to push unsuccessfully for the banning of coal refineries.) And they had no clue that there was a potential gold mine in the stuff they were throwing away.

"The thing with naphtha was no one knew what to do with it," Heller says. Then along came the internal-combustion engine, which required an explosive fuel that would be ignited by spark plugs. That meant gasoline, which was produced with naphtha—and the rest is history.

But there's nothing more in that history about Ponsi, leaving some tantalizing questions unanswered. Was he an ingenious businessman, finding riches in the by-products of others' work, or the predecessor of those folks we see wandering around today, filling shopping carts with other people's trash? The image that comes to my mind is of a farmer in hell, wandering through oily lagoons to harvest the putrid fields of industry.

Perhaps the world will never know any more about Ponsi,

but Sylvia Hunt has now been given her due, mainly because of Heller's curiosity.

During the late 1870s, Hunt owned a refinery at Fleet and Eden streets near Fells Point. At the time, Rockefeller's Standard Oil was buying up and consolidating Baltimore refineries. Alone among her peers, Hunt tried to dictate the terms of her sale to the powerful oil monopoly—unsuccessfully, as it turned out. Standard, with control of the market, limited the supply of crude oil to Hunt's facility. Eventually, she tired of the pressure and left the business, and the refinery ended up in Standard Oil's hands after all. Hunt was able to survive—barely—by eventually opening up another refinery that produced paraffin, a solid mixture of hydrocarbons used primarily in candles and sealing materials. She lived into her 90s.

Hunt's tale caught the attention of legendary muckraker Ida M. Tarbell, whose 1904 *McClure's* magazine article, "The History of the Standard Oil Company," led to the landmark U.S. Supreme Court decision in 1911 to dissolve the behemoth company. But beyond that, history barely remembered the gutsy and pioneering businesswoman. Heller's resurrection of Hunt's story (he wrote an article about her in 1992 for the Maryland Historical Society's magazine) shows what one curious person can do to make history more than a mere chronology.

Why did he go to the trouble? "I knew it was a good story," Heller shrugs. He also knew that history is limited, too often fixated on toting up the winners and regurgitating the flat facts, when sometimes the stories of the strugglers at the fringes—the Ponsis and the Sylvia Hunts—can offer a better glimpse into the times in which they lived.

Charles Cohen
September 8, 1999

Free Press

Baltimore in the 1820s should have been fertile ground for the anti-slavery movement. A fourth of the city's residents were of African descent, and most of these were "free" blacks, whose numbers rose from 8,000 in 1820 to 15,000 in 1830. There was also a core group of whites, mostly Quakers, who were active in opposing slavery.

Still, while free blacks owned homes and built churches, they couldn't vote or sit on juries. And although slavery was on the decline throughout Maryland, Baltimore remained entangled in the slave-based economy. Thousands of slaves, chiefly domestic servants and shipyard workers, still labored here.

In 1824, a Quaker named Benjamin Lundy entered the picture. Lundy had been wandering from state to state, preaching against slavery and distributing a self-published newspaper called *The Genius of Universal Emancipation*. He wanted a permanent home for his monthly periodical, and Baltimore offered a desirable mid-Atlantic location.

Mobtown didn't exactly welcome Lundy. He was physically assaulted by slave-trader Austin Woolfolk, and a Baltimore judge attempted to put him out of business on phony libel charges. Stubbornly, Lundy decided in 1829 to publish *The Genius* on a weekly basis. To assist him, he recruited a 24-year-old editor from Massachusetts who had already distinguished himself as an eloquent advocate of political and social reform.

William Lloyd Garrison, a largely self-educated writer and printer, had met Lundy two years before in Boston and been inspired by the Quaker's righteous fixation on the slavery question. However, they differed in their approach to the issue: Lundy advocated a pragmatic, gradual dismantling of the slave system; Garrison called for immediate emancipation.

Garrison moved to Baltimore itching for controversy. For

The Genius he wrote signed editorials that were far more confrontational than Lundy's, and he compiled a weekly column of "horrible news" items concerning slavery.

In November 1829, while Lundy was out of town, Garrison learned that a shipment of 75 slaves had just left Maryland for New Orleans. The ship's owner was Francis Todd, a merchant from Garrison's hometown of Newburyport, Massachusetts; the deal had been brokered by Lundy's old nemesis, Austin Woolfolk. Garrison went on the attack, declaring that merchants such as Todd should be "sentenced to solitary confinement for life" and accusing the ship's captain, Nicholas Brown, of "domestic piracy."

Todd sued for libel. The trial began on March 1, 1830, in the brick courthouse that stood at the corner of Calvert and Lexington streets, present site of the Clarence M. Mitchell Jr. Courthouse. Nicholas Brice, the judge who had tangled with Lundy a few years before, presided. A jury of 12 white men took 15 minutes to convict Garrison. He was sentenced to serve six months in jail or pay a $50 fine plus court costs.

Garrison chose jail, prompting the judge to grumble that the defendant seemed "ambitious of becoming a martyr." As it turned out, the jail experience was relatively cushy. The warden, a reformer named David Hudson, didn't want to throw the young offender in with street thugs, so he kept Garrison at his own residence on the grounds of the jail. Garrison, describing himself as "snug as a robin in a cage," used the time to write an account of the libel trial, which Lundy published as a pamphlet. He also interviewed recaptured runaway slaves, wrote poetry, and sent taunting letters to Brice and Todd.

The pamphlet was read by a wealthy sympathizer from New York, who subsequently paid Garrison's fines and court costs. On June 5, after 49 days in jail, the unrepentant scribe walked free. He and Lundy had already ended their editorial partnership, amicably, after the libel conviction. Garrison, galvanized by his new notoriety, returned to Boston, where, on January 1, 1831, he launched *The Liberator*, which would become the flagship newspaper of the anti-slavery cause for the next 34 years. (The full story is told in Henry Mayer's *All on Fire*, a lively biography of Garrison published in 1998 by St. Martin's Press.)

Thus Baltimore lost its chance to become the wellspring of the abolitionist movement. Perhaps the city wasn't prepared for the mantle anyway. In 1835, a small group of distinguished free-black Baltimoreans published an open letter denouncing Garrison and his newly formed American Anti-Slavery Society as "mistaken, hot-headed zealots" bent on plunging the country into war.

Tom Chalkley
October 20, 1999

Charmed People

Waxing Historic

As an 11-year-old gathering firewood near his home in Gram, North Carolina, Gene Stinnette ran into two white teenagers who grabbed him and threw a rope over a tree branch. "At that age, I thought they were playing with me," he recalls. "You never know what would have happened." If not for the intervention of an old man who lived in a nearby cabin, Stinnette's name might have been among the 500 memorialized in the Great Blacks in Wax museum's exhibit on lynching.

Stinnette, now 65, says he repressed the memory for years; it came flooding back a few months ago as he and Great Blacks in Wax president Elmer Martin were putting together a gruesome exhibit of a husband-and-wife lynching. As the North Avenue institution's chief set-builder, Stinnette has had his share of personal confrontations with history.

A city maintenance mechanic on loan to the museum, Stinnette combines the ingenuity to use a soap dispenser as an astronaut's air pack with the strength to lift a 375-pound rock. Elmer Martin calls him a "godsend"; Martin's wife, museum executive director Joanne Martin, nicknamed Stinnette "Super Hammer."

Eight years ago, Stinnette saw the museum as a side job, a place to pick up some extra money doing maintenance work in his off hours. Then the museum asked him to rehab the building's top floor into what is now the Maryland Room, featuring exhibits on local African-Americans. "After I read some of the literature, I thought it was something worthwhile," he says. He began going to the museum when his city shift ended at 4 p.m., often working there until midnight. In June 1996, the city took him off regular maintenance duty and stationed him at Great Blacks.

Stinnette's workshop is located in what was once the embalming room of a funeral home at the east end of the 1600 block of North Avenue. (The museum proper is in a former fire hall at the west end of the block.) Rows of drill presses line the walls. Choice tools are displayed over a green-brick fireplace. From this cozy room, Stinnette writes history large, using minimal materials to create the museum's message-heavy effect. Eubie Blake's piano was made from plywood. The space capsule in the exhibit honoring Guion Bluford and Mae Jemison, the country's first African-American male and female astronauts, was built from the old Memorial Stadium scoreboard, with computer parts, lights, and circuits Stinnette found in a trash container when he was part of the city crew preparing the stadium for use by the Baltimore Stallions.

Stinnette says he never works from drawings; he simply gathers his materials and gets down to it. "It's like a picture coming in my mind that had already been drawn," he says.

His most ambitious accomplishment is still in progress—a slave-ship exhibit he began in 1992 that will ultimately stretch across several buildings in the 1600 block of North. (The museum is expanding from its present location through the intervening rowhouses to the building that houses Stinnette's workshop.) He used a sledgehammer and chisel to bash through a 31-inch stone wall from the current museum building into the basement of the neighboring rowhouse, which now serves as the bowels of a ship, where a cargo of slaves moans in agony. He plans to expand the exhibit into the next house down; that space will serve as the African coast, from which viewers will observe the ship.

Like many of those the museum celebrates, Stinnette has overcome heavy odds and heartbreak. When he was 14, his father was killed in a bar fight. (Stinnette says his father's last conversation with him was a lecture about staying out late.) Stinnette subsequently dropped out of school and got a job cleaning car upholstery. He married at 17 and had five children, the oldest of whom was shot to death in 1982 at the age of 30. In 1961 his first wife died of a cerebral hemorrhage. He remarried and had three more children, one of whom died of leukemia.

Stinnette learned his trade in the 1950s by rehabbing his home and doing work for neighbors. Hired by the city in 1972 as a custodian, he moved up the ranks to become a maintenance mechanic, doing plumbing, locksmithing, and basic building repairs. (An eighth-degree black belt in karate, he has also worked as a martial-arts instructor for the city's Recreation and Parks Department.) These days he's passing on his skills to one of his sons, 23-year-old Remun, hoping to keep the museum work in the family.

"Truthfully, when I came over here [to Great Blacks in Wax] I knew very, very little on history," he says. "But since I've been up here I have been enlightened a lot. There's a lot that I have learned and a lot that I am learning."

Charles Cohen
April 1, 1998

Postscript: Gene Stinnette still works at the Great Blacks in Wax Museum. The lynching and African-coast exhibits have been completed.

Blow Up

It's easy to spot Bubbie the Balloon Man wheeling his cart through Fells Point. Sometimes he's sitting down at the wharf near Piccolo's. Other times he can be seen standing, a bit winded, in front of a grocery store. He's hard to miss.

He wears a 3-foot-high puffy hat, wrap-around shades, and a stylized sports jacket that looks like it could have been peeled from a wing-back chair. He has gray stubble and doesn't smile much. Then again, Bubbie, also known as Leon Fox, doesn't

have much to smile about, to hear him tell it.

At 68, he is burdened with a slew of ailments, from asthma, to large splinters in his leg that routinely send him to the hospital for operations, to arthritis in his hands that's nagging him to get out of the balloon business. He's on Social Security but earns extra income making animal- and flower-shaped balloons for tourists, kids, lovers, drunks—whoever ambles by and wants one.

Normally such a trade requires a certain amount of spunk—some goofy slapstick perhaps, or at least a little clown talk. Bubbie's shtick is that he doesn't have one—or, perhaps, he has what might be called anti-shtick.

"Don't break them, honey," he fires at a little girl who toddles up to his cart and reaches for a Tigger balloon. "Don't touch them. Don't play with them. You break it, you pay for it."

So the balloons are left to sell themselves. The only problem is, it's a buck for the animals, two for the flowers. Upon hearing the prices, one kid holding his sister's hand blinks at the sight of a sagging dachshund and keeps walking.

"They think that because they're balloons you're supposed to give 'em away for nothing," Fox says. "They don't realize I pay big money for this stuff." He pats his fanny pack stuffed with balloons and two hand pumps. He talks constantly about his street-performance license, and the fact that he still can't get an OK to work the city's premier street-performance venue, Harborplace. But despite his troubles and complaints, he takes pride in his work.

"I'm not a balloon man," he says. "I'm a balloon sculptor. I make something that looks like what I say it is. When I make a dinosaur, it looks like a dinosaur. When I make Tigger, people know it's Tigger. When I make a poodle dog, it looks like a poodle dog."

Fox's show-biz roots go back to his father, who worked as a circus roustabout before dying from tuberculosis at 30. Fox and his sisters, who grew up on Wolfe Street just a few blocks from his current stomping grounds, ended up orphaned. After being passed around from an orphanage on a farm in Dorsey to St. Mary's Industrial School (now Cardinal Gibbons High School), Fox joined Ringling Brothers, where he held a variety of jobs. For the next 15 years he would crisscross the country on trains, setting up the big tops for Ringling Brothers and other circuses. He met the world's most famous clown, Emmett Kelly.

"They would show me a few things, little odds and ends—I can make things disappear," he says, glancing away behind his clunky windshield shades on a cloudy day.

But Fox never had any desire to get into the performance end of the business. He was happy enough setting up, and then sitting in the highest seat in the big top and working the lights. "The show couldn't start without me," he says.

His life changed in the late '50s when he fell 65 feet from the high wire onto concrete at Soldier's Field in Chicago. Hitting some wires on the way down slowed his fall and saved his life, but he spent the next three years in a traction bed and was told he would never walk again. He proved the doctors wrong. After regaining the use of his legs, he came back to Baltimore, where he did a variety of odd jobs before settling with a vending company, where he worked for 23 years.

Five years ago Fox saw a man making balloon animals; he figured he could handle that and could pick up some extra cash. He says on good days he makes about $75. "I'm considered one of the best, if not the best," he says. But between the asthma and the splinters, Fox wonders how long he can keep it up. Right now he just goes out on weekends, for a few hours before his ailments send him back home.

On Memorial Day weekend the Inner Harbor is thick with tourists. But in Fells Point the herd has thinned considerably. Bubbie is sitting dockside. The afternoon heat is popping his inflated display. Two little girls and their parents are waiting for their flower balloons. It's as wholesome a scene as you can imagine. Fox is telling them how he was shot once in a bar. As Fox tells the story, he twists the flower balloon too tight and it pops. The family gazes at him, perplexed. He looks at the customers and changes the subject. He'll make them a rare balloon, he says—no one makes the blue flowers anymore. The girls get their balloons, the father smiles politely, and they walk away.

Charles Cohen
June 19, 1998

Excuse Her Dust

It was annoyance that brought Dorothy Parker, famed Manhattan author and wit, to Baltimore once in 1924. On a train from New York to Wilmington, Delaware, for a production of her latest play, Parker was obliged to share a parlor car with an actress who chattered the entire trip. As the cast disembarked in Wilmington, an exasperated Parker turned

to two colleagues and said, "Let's go to Baltimore."

Arriving that evening, the threesome looked up H.L. Mencken, who invited them to dinner and drinks. Mencken had published several of Parker's stories in his magazine *Smart Set*, but as the evening wore on, his racist jokes offended her so much that she took a midnight train back to Wilmington.

The story captures three of Parker's lifelong traits: spontaneity, impatience with fools, and an abiding antipathy toward racism. By a twist of fate, it was her passion for racial equality that brought her back to Baltimore—for keeps.

Although Parker was a prolific writer of prose, criticism, and screenplays, she is chiefly remembered today for a handful of wisecracks and clever rhymes. Her politics are largely forgotten, perhaps because in that arena she was more inclined toward action than words. She was arrested in 1927 while protesting the execution of anarchists Nicola Sacco and

Bartolomeo Vanzetti. In the 1930s she raised money to help defend the Scottsboro Boys, a group of black youths accused of raping a white girl. As fascism gained ground in Europe, Parker (whose father was Jewish) denounced the Nazis and supported the anti-Franco forces in the Spanish Civil War. In the '40s, she helped organize a screenwriters' union; in the '50s, redbaiting destroyed her Hollywood career. For the rest of her life she kept her politics pretty much to herself.

When friends persuaded Parker in 1964 to write a will, she decided to leave her estate, including rights to her work, to Martin Luther King Jr., whose "I have a dream" speech was still ringing in the nation's ears. The will called for the money to be transferred to the National Association for the Advancement of Colored People (NAACP) if King should die. Parker chose her friend and fellow playwright Lillian Hellman as her literary executor.

Parker died June 7, 1967. King, who had never met her, was surprised by her bequest, which netted him $20,448.39. He took it as a sign that "the Lord will provide." Parker was cremated; the ashes, on Hellman's instructions, were mailed to the law offices of O'Dwyer and Bernstien, the firm that drew up Parker's will. King was assassinated less than a year later, and the estate—including rights to Parker's written work—was passed on to the NAACP.

The biographical details related here up to this point are cribbed from the biography *Dorothy Parker: What Fresh Hell Is This?* by Marion Meade, published in 1988. But there's more to the story.

For 20 years Parker's ashes remained in a file cabinet at O'Dwyer and Bernstien. In the late 1980s this fact, reported in Meade's book, came to the attention of Benjamin Hooks, then the NAACP's executive director, by way of Liz Smith's gossip column. Meeting with a group of Parker's admirers at the Algonquin Hotel, Parker's legendary hangout in New York, Hooks suggested the ashes be interred at the civil-rights group's new national headquarters, a former Trappist monastery on

Mount Hope Road in Northwest Baltimore.

At a ceremony in October 1988, Parker's remains were interred in a grove of white pines on the NAACP grounds, beneath a round brass plate set within three concentric circles of brick. The inscription includes the epitaph Parker once suggested for herself—EXCUSE MY DUST—and alludes, poignantly, to "the bonds of everlasting friendship between Black and Jewish people."

"We get calls every now and then" about the little shrine, says James Murray, librarian at the NAACP headquarters. "People who move here from New York City call and ask if it's OK to visit." It is. And like another of Baltimore's permanent residents, Edgar Allan Poe, Parker has a mysterious annual visitor.

"Each year, on her birthday," Murray says, "someone leaves a martini and a rose."

Tom Chalkley
August 26, 1998

The Courtroom Kidnapper

A lot of folks today will tell you politicians are criminals. Usually they're referring to supposed indiscretions committed while in office. In the case of one storied Baltimore pol, though, a law-skirting adventure the local media dubbed a "kidnapping" was the spark that ignited a nearly 30-year political career.

The story starts not with the kidnapping, but with a murder. On August 18, 1922, three men attacked William B. Norris, a well-known local contractor, and his bookkeeper as they walked along Madison Avenue, carrying some $7,000 in payroll money from their bank to their office. Norris was shot dead. The robbers held a rapidly forming crowd at bay at gunpoint until a waiting getaway car with three other men inside picked the scofflaws up and sped off.

The brazen daylight slaying gripped the city. Rewards totaling $10,000 were offered for capture of the killers. Three of the five suspects were nabbed in Baltimore within five days; another was caught in Washington, D.C. The fifth, Walter Socolow, fled to New York; he was arrested, reportedly, when he emerged from his hideout to buy an out-of-town paper to catch up on the news back home.

City officials sought to have the 19-year-old Socolow extradited to Baltimore to stand trial. It should have been a routine process; New York's governor had signed the extradition papers and, according to newspaper accounts, Socolow was willing to come back to Baltimore and spill his guts. Herbert R. O'Conor, a 25-year-old assistant state's attorney, was sent by his boss to retrieve the prisoner.

Arriving in New York, the Maryland attorney instead found himself in the middle of a legal standoff. Socolow had changed his mind about returning voluntarily and was claiming he had been in New York on August 18. His lawyers were filing writs of habeas corpus in an effort to delay the proceedings, and a New York judge was refusing to OK the extradition without evidence linking Socolow to the crime.

On September 21, O'Conor and two Baltimore detectives sat in a New York courtroom as arguments over the defense motion stretched on. Tension was mounting; this was a big story back home in Baltimore, big enough that the young prosecutor's father, prominent hotelier James P.A. O'Conor, had made a trip to New York to see his son at work. In the meantime, an *Evening Sun* reporter covering the proceedings had heard about defense plans to continue the delaying tactics, and tipped Herbert O'Conor off.

As the judge banged down his gavel, dismissing one of the

habeas corpus writs, O'Conor and the detectives rushed forward. They grabbed Socolow and, with the *Sun* man in tow, sprinted out of the courtroom. As the judge yelled for them to stop, they ran out of the courthouse and into a car that the New York Police Department had furnished them as a courtesy, little suspecting how it was to be used. The fugitives drove to the nearest ferry, crossed into New Jersey, and hopped on a train to Baltimore.

The New York judge was miffed and the NYPD embarrassed, but in Baltimore a star was born. The Socolow apprehension made national news, and the hometown papers made a celebrity of the daring prosecutor: "O'Conor Tells How Socolow Returned," ran one headline (which also offered the Baltimorean's caveat: "Didn't Hear Judge Cry Out"). The previously unheralded assistant state's attorney "became the shining hero...in the nick of time," historian Harry W. Kirwin wrote in his O'Conor biography, *The Inevitable Success*.

From there, it was a short step into the public life. "Because of the notoriety and the publicity, he went into local politics, and from that [came] his political career," says Jim O'Conor, Herbert O'Conor's son and president of the real-estate firm O'Conor, Piper, and Flynn. Local Democrats began talking Herbert up for office. In 1923, at the tender age of 27, he was elected Baltimore's state's attorney. In 1934 he was elected Maryland's attorney general, and he captured the governorship four years later. After two terms in the State House, O'Conor was voted into the U.S. Senate, serving one term before various problems, including a heart condition, forced him to retire. He died in his native Baltimore on March 4, 1960, at the age of 63.

The political acumen that carried O'Conor to victory in every election he ever entered was duly noted by the commentators of his day, who didn't forget the smashing case that put him on the map. "Usually O'Conor's opportunism has been skillfully timed," *Sun* columnist E.T. Baker III wrote in 1943, "as in his kidnapping of a Baltimore gunman from a New York City courtroom, a melodramatic escapade which first brought him to the attention of the voters." Today, the name of the man who kidnapped his way into the spotlight is emblazoned on a state office building at Martin Luther King Jr. Boulevard and Howard Street.

Charles Cohen
September 2, 1998

Ms. Hi-De-Ho

The song was "Minnie the Moocher." If anybody should have known the words, it was the co-composer, Cab Calloway, the famed entertainer who grew up in West Baltimore. But during a 1931 performance at Harlem's Cotton Club, Cab's mind went blank. He forgot the lyrics mid-song. In front of a live audience, the show—and the music—had to go on. Without missing a beat he sang "hi-de-hi-de-hi-de-ho," then "ho-de-ho-de-ho-de-hee." His life would never be the same again.

Cab Calloway became known as the "hi-de-ho man," but perhaps less known is that there was also a "hi-de-ho woman." Cab was a big-time big-band leader—but also a little brother. Indeed, if it weren't for his older sister Blanche, he might have become a lawyer. Not only did big sis help to start his show biz career, she showed him the way through her own success.

Blanche Calloway was a bandleader, singer, and dancer in her own right. This "Queen of Hi-De-Ho" toured the country and cut records. Her talents rivaled Cab's, but her story is rarely told.

Unlike Cab (who was born during the Calloway family's stay in Rochester, New York), Blanche was born in Baltimore, about 1901. She grew up on Druid Hill Avenue and later on Carey Street. She had a good voice as a girl, and was encouraged to sing by her musical mother, Eulalia. Blanche studied at Morgan College (today, Morgan State University), but around 1921 she opted for a show-business career, joining the traveling act Oma Crosby and Her Five Cubanolas. (Blanche doused herself with various skin-lightening powders to look Latina rather than African-American.) While in New York, she landed a spot in *Shuffle Along* (with Josephine Baker), the hit Broadway revue with music by Baltimore's own Eubie Blake. By 1928 she was in the Chicago-based traveling show *Plantation Days*.

The details of how a teenage Cab came to join Blanche in Chicago are somewhat murky. In his 1976 autobiography, *Of Minnie the Moocher & Me*, Cab wrote that Blanche helped him get a part in *Plantation Days* when it played in Baltimore, and he followed the show back to Chicago. Blanche's own published accounts say she was simply visiting her family in Baltimore and took Cab back to Chicago with her. (The ostensible reason was so Cab could go to college, but he had been playing the drums in a Baltimore jazz combo and was eager to follow Blanche into show biz.) Cab started studying law in the Windy City, but through his sister's contacts he also began singing in clubs and working his way up the musical ladder. (A star basketball player at Frederick Douglass High School, Cab was also offered a spot on the Harlem Globetrotters. Blanche talked him out of it.)

After Cab's career eclipsed Blanche's, she began to sing with his band. But in 1931 she assumed leadership of her own outfit: Blanche Calloway and Her Twelve Clouds of Joy. For the next 13 years, through the heart of the swing era, Blanche toured, recorded, and jammed as the first and most famous lady bandleader. Many a top player did time with her group, including Ben Webster and Clyde Hart. She is said to have purchased Cozy Cole his first set of drums.

Blanche quit show biz cold turkey in 1944. (It was good timing—the big-band era was in its waning days.) But this pioneering woman didn't go quietly into retirement. In the '50s she worked for Miami radio station WMBM, becoming one of the South's first female disc jockeys. Then she started the first mail-order cosmetics business for black women. Having experienced rabid racism firsthand (while touring with the band in Mississippi she was arrested for using a whites-only ladies room), she became active in the civil-rights movement.

When the time for quiet retirement did come, Blanche spent it back in her native Baltimore, in a ranch house near Lake Montebello. She passed away in 1978. (The CD compilation *Blanche Calloway 1923-1935* by Blanche Calloway and Her Joy Boys keeps her music alive in the digital age.)

While Blanche often dismissed her musical skills, famed pianist and composer Earl "Fatha" Hines thought she was the better-sounding Calloway, writing in his autobiography that "all of [Cab's] style was hers." For his part, Cab never forgot Blanche's role in his fame, dedicating his autobiography to the big sister "who introduced me to the wonderful world of entertainment."

Brennen Jensen
September 9, 1998

Fish Story

Just above a dam in Dickeyville, Gwynns Falls forms a deep, silty pool that is full of hidden life. Bubbles rise from the blurry bottom. "Probably a turtle," Joseph Barnhart says. Soon enough, a young snapping turtle drifts to the surface and lazes awhile before sliding back into the murk. Then there's a slapping sound, and ripples spread from a spot in the middle of the water. "You missed that," Mike Womack says. "A smallmouth came up and smacked that grasshopper."

Having spent good chunks of their lives fishing Gwynns Falls, Barnhart and Womack share a deep affection for this urban waterway. Womack, who first fished the stream as a child in the early '70s, remembers a time when Dickeyville neighbors would spend entire summer days virtually camped out on its banks with baited hooks.

Barnhart started fishing Gwynns Falls in 1984. "You can't really enjoy this stream till you walk it," he declares. "You get a wholly different perspective." He revels in the stream's wildlife, and worries about its polluted water.

Both men live in Woodlawn—Barnhart's a mechanic and Womack's a plumber—but they seem surprised to be asked about their homes and jobs. They'd rather talk about fishing.

Womack fly-fishes exclusively and winds his own lures; Barnhart prefers a short rod and a light line. They and a few like-minded friends have explored Gwynns Falls from Scotts Level Branch in Randallstown to Wilkens Avenue in the city, pulling out smallmouth bass, pumpkinseeds, bluegills, warmouth ("the most aggressive of the sunfish," Barnhart says), blue and bullhead catfish, rainbow and brook trout, and—near Wilkens Avenue—"monster" suckers, some 3 feet long. Along the way they've encountered creatures you don't think of as typical urban wildlife: beavers right on the city line, for example, or the snapping turtle Barnhart once saw overturned on a roadside by the stream that was so huge "it took three men to turn it over."

Neither man has read *The Compleat Angler*, Izaak Walton's 17th-century classic on the "contemplative man's entertainment," but they've lived it. "When I get stressed out at work," Barnhart says, "I grab my fishing rod and come down to the stream. I don't even need to catch anything. I'm just doing what I love doing." Womack says he fishes for "the quietness... and the smallmouth."

All the fish they catch are returned to the water; neither man risks eating them. Barnhart blames sewer-line leaks for foul smells and parasite-infested fish. "Every smallmouth you pull out will have eight to 10 parasites in the meat," he says, describing yellow worms that squish like water balloons. The other big pollution source is runoff—trash and toxins swept from the vast pavements of the Gwynns Falls watershed into the stream. "In the '80s there weren't so many of these plastic bags that they give out at grocery stores," Barnhart says. "I see a lot more of 'em stuck in trees and caught under rocks. You get one of those bags with an air bubble in it, and a turtle will go for that. There's no way a turtle can digest a plastic bag."

Pollution, they say, is only part of the problem. Runoff from hot streets makes the water too warm for some native fish. Barriers, like the dam that creates the pond in Gwynn Oaks Park, thwart the upstream spawning instincts of a number of important species.

One of the state's strategies for boosting fish populations is to stock streams with farm-raised fish—especially popular sport fish such as rainbow trout. But the practice puzzles Womack and Barnhart, who feel it sends a misleading message: "You put rainbow trout in there, a lot of people think it's OK to eat," Womack says.

The two anglers are more positive about plans to revive Gwynns Falls and Leakin Park with a trail system, campgrounds, and other attractions. Fishing, Barnhart says, could offer city kids an alternative to street life, "if somebody takes the time and shows them how." Still, they worry about safety in some of the park's lonelier reaches: They've seen drugs, guns, and prostitutes downstream. Womack once found a dead body. That's the kind of wilderness experience nobody needs.

Tom Chalkley
September 23, 1998

For the Birds

Nobody responds to the doorbell of this gray bungalow, but there's no doubt I've come to the right house. There is an answer of sorts to the ringing: The squawk, shriek, and whistle of birds is discernible even on the doorstep outside. And of all the houses in the modest neighborhood, this is the only one with cages stacked on the porch. No question about it: I've found the home of Gerda Deterer—the Bird Lady of Dundalk.

A green Oldsmobile station wagon soon pulls up to the curb. Deterer—all 5 feet of her—slides out and explains she had an emergency call about a wounded animal. She scurries to the back of the wagon, where something is wrapped in a pillow case—something that quickly gets hold of her finger. "The people said it was a parrot on the phone," she says, wincing at the pinch and shaking her head. "It's a sharp-shinned hawk. Sometimes we get people saying they have a hawk and it turns

out to be a pigeon—we get some strange calls sometimes."

Deterer eventually pulls a beautiful brown-and-white bird of prey from the cloth. It may have a fractured wing—only an X-ray will tell for sure. She gingerly carries the animal to the cages on the cramped porch, which already houses two caged opossums and a collection of convalescing pigeons.

Still more cages crowd Deterer's living room. A pair of cockatoos emit playful "hellos" and ear-bursting shrieks. We retreat back outside to talk about how this 57-year-old erstwhile pastry baker came to devote all her waking hours to aiding and abetting wounded wildlife.

It all began, Deterer explains, some 25 years ago with an injured robin she, er, took under her wing. With advice from the Baltimore Zoo she nursed the bird back to health—and along the way came to realize that while there were many local organizations helping dogs and cats, few aided wild animals. She began to take in other wounded wild things, eventually learning enough to become a state-licensed wildlife rehabilitator. In 1994 she founded Wild Bird Rescue Inc., a nonprofit association of volunteers dedicated to looking after injured birds and other small creatures. It's an arduous task that presents new challenges with each passing month. "In March we'll start getting overpowered by baby squirrels," she says. "Then come the baby bunnies. In April and May come the baby birds, and your life stops."

Young birds need to be fed every 20 minutes, and Wild Bird Rescue might take in 50 young birds a season. Of course, some untrained folks may try to help orphaned baby birds on their own. Deterer says these would-be good Samaritans often do more harm than good. The task is best left to skilled rehabilitators, who not only know how to best assist the animals, but also can prepare them for a return to their natural habitat.

"You can't cuddle the birds," she says. "You don't want them to think people are their friends. The birds need to survive on their own in the wild."

Deterer's group now has some 52 members, including a number of dedicated veterinarians who perform the more serious medical procedures, sometimes pro bono (though the group almost always has to pay for X-rays and medicine). She also works closely with the Carrie Murray Outdoor Education Center in Leakin Park. This is where the "big guys" (the owls, hawks, and eagles) are coaxed back to health.

In just five years, Wild Bird Rescue has tended to an amazing menagerie of critters, from hawks, herons, and hummingbirds to a host of small mammals and reptiles. Once, it even took in some baby armadillos, though Deterer still doesn't know how these southern creatures got to Baltimore. The group doesn't discriminate—pigeons and starlings receive the same care as the rarest owl. (As Deterer says, "Everything hurts and everything bleeds.")

There are, however, a number of creatures that the Maryland Department of Natural Resources forbids Wild Bird

Rescue to assist, including foxes, raccoons, beavers, skunks, bobcats, and otters. Due to concerns over rabies, Maryland is one of the few states that euthanizes, rather than rehabilitates, these animals when they become wounded or sick.

"We don't agree with this at all," Deterer says, downplaying the rabies threat. "If rehabilitators can't help, the public might do it themselves, putting people at a higher risk."

Working to change this law and educating the general populace on the proper handling of wounded wildlife are also parts of Wild Bird Rescue's purview. But like most volunteer-run nonprofits, the group's ambitions often outstrip its finances. This year, Deterer says it may spend $22,000 caring for critters. (Formula alone for young squirrels and rabbits runs into the thousands of dollars.) Much of Wild Bird Rescue's funding comes from small donations, though it has received financial assistance from national groups including the Animal Welfare League and a $5,000 grant from the William Snyder Foundation for Animals. Recently, a Carroll County woman donated 45 acres of land near Finksburg to the group. Deterer envisions building a proper wildlife hospital and rehabilitation center on the site, complete with the large pens necessary to help ease animals back into nature. But first she needs to find funding for the project.

Meanwhile, the Bird Lady of Dundalk keeps busy answering calls about wounded animals—doing her best to undo the damage of their harsh encounters with the modern, man-made world.

"When you watch an animal return to the wild—that's the moment." Deterer says, blissfully. "It feels wonderful."

Brennen Jensen
December 9, 1998

Postscipt: Gerda Deterer and her team of volunteers are still looking after wounded and orphaned critters, and trying to raise money for their *wildlife-rehabilitation center. The project will cost $200,000 and fundraising is going slowly, but Deterer promises, "It's going to happen."*

Holy Spirit

The Rev. Richard Lawrence lights his pipe. Sweet-smelling smoke wafts around his robust, bearded face, which is already peering hungrily into the tin of tobacco, looking for more. He waves the match in the air and talks—about politics, class, urban struggles, his love of food—before tossing the spent stick onto a box of old newspapers.

Not the most prudent move, perhaps, but nothing ignites. The pastor of St. Vincent de Paul Church in Jonestown knows when the time is right to start a fire.

Lawrence is sitting in his parish house, a three-story federal-style home that's dwarfed by the neighboring 159-year-old church building. Later, strolling through the wing that connects the two buildings, he seems a figure of splendid isolation; the image of a lighthouse watchman comes to mind. But it's just that, an image—this priest is nothing if not engaged with the world, and not just on Sundays. He takes his cue from Jesus—the rebel.

"I look at it this way," Lawrence says, pausing for effect. "I get a check once a month, whether I need it, deserve it, or not, to be a professional disciple of a man who was executed as a rabble-rouser. If I'm not causing trouble for a bureaucrat somewhere I should be ashamed to cash my check."

Signs of Lawrence's leanings are all around his home. Along with traditional icons and pictures of the pope, there's a menorah in a corner of his office, and in the hallway is a painting of a man holding a Torah. In the dining room is a large painting of Jesus by Baltimore artist John H.T. Neal Jr. This Jesus has a racially ambiguous skin tone, bulked-up arms, and a belly that, as Lawrence puts it, looks "four months pregnant." The skyline depicted behind Jesus is of Baltimore, not Jerusalem. Over his head are the words POLOCK, WOP, NIGGER, KIKE.

The painting's point, Lawrence says, is that if Jesus were alive today, He'd be hanging out with the poor and oppressed. The image may be shocking, but given Lawrence's own ministry, it's hardly surprising to find it in his home.

Jonestown, located just east of the southern end of Interstate 83, was founded in 1732, 65 years before Baltimore City was incorporated. In its early days, the neighborhood was home to the elite, including the Carrolls, one of the nation's richest families. Over the years, it was claimed by Irish, Italian, and Jewish immigrants, and became progressively poorer, according to records at the city's Commission for Historical and Architectural Preservation. By the time the Lafayette Courts and Flag House projects were built in the 1950s, much of Jonestown was considered a slum, and more recently the drug trade put a stranglehold on the community.

Lawrence came to St. Vincent de Paul in 1973 as a veteran of the civil-rights battles of the '60s, marching on local businesses that discriminated against African-Americans. When the Rev. Martin Luther King Jr. was assassinated and Baltimore erupted in riots, Lawrence joined other clergy and civil-rights leaders out in the streets, trying to quell the violence.

In 1974 he organized the Jonestown Planning Council, of which he remains president today. The council has pushed for a neighborhood-revitalization plan, established a day-care center for neighborhood children, recruited businesses that could use city funding to rehab old storefronts, and supported the opening of a center for homeless veterans and housing for AIDS sufferers.

Not only has Lawrence been a community voice, he has also been a rallying force for other local activists. "Before Father Lawrence, we residents of Flag House weren't listened to," says Irona Pope, a neighborhood activist for 35 years and co-organizer of a community food cooperative.

Lawrence, Pope and others say, taught residents how to organize to meet common goals and hold city officials accountable for unkept promises. Most importantly, he helped unify the fractured communities of Lafayette Courts and Flag House when the city started talking about razing the old housing projects. "He's always on the front lines when it comes to issues involving City Hall," says Dwight Warren, executive director of Jonestown's McKim Community Center.

At early discussions with Lafayette Court tenants, Baltimore Housing Commissioner Daniel Henson recalls, Lawrence would be the lone white person in the room—and one of the most aggressive advocates for the all-minority community. "He would come to the community meetings and had very strong opinions [on issues involving the housing projects] for a white man," Henson says. "Literally everyone in the community knew and trusted him and gave him respect. From the second meeting on we took his opinions very seriously."

Henson got to see just how serious Lawrence could be when the American Civil Liberties Union filed suit against the city in 1995 over segregation in the housing projects. The suit would have temporarily blocked the demolition of the high-rises. Lawrence and the Jonestown Planning Council, who wanted to see the buildings razed, obtained a pro-bono lawyer and filed a brief on behalf of the city. The priest also pushed Henson to allow some of the homes built to replace Lafayette Courts to be set aside for home ownership rather than as subsidized or rental housing. Now, 10 percent of the homes in Pleasant View Gardens, which rose after Lafayette Courts were torn down, are owner-occupied.

Asked about why he has taken on the role of neighborhood activist rather than simply spiritual adviser, Lawrence again puffs on the pipe, producing a thick cloud of smoke. He tells a story about planting trees with his elderly father.

"I said, 'Dad, why are you putting so much energy into planting these scrawny little things?' He looked at me and said, 'Son, if I sit in the shade of a tree I did not plant, then I shall plant a tree in the shade [of which] I will not sit.' So I got some trees to plant."

Charles Cohen
January 13, 1999

Postscript: The Rev. Richard Lawrence remains pastor at St. Vincent de Paul and an active community leader in Jonestown, recently helping broker deals with the Baltimore Development Corporation to ensure that businesses recruited to move into the area will hire locally.

The Odd Father

It's not for nothing that our burg is billed as the Monumental City. Baltimore is generously dotted with marble, granite, and bronze statues and memorials to historical figures and fave sons and daughters—everyone from Robert E. Lee to Billie Holiday. East Baltimore's Broadway is tantamount to a monumental row, so many marble and metal tributes does it sport.

Just south of Broadway's junction with Fayette Street, at perhaps the boulevard's loftiest point, perches a particularly monumental monument: a soaring, fluted column crowned with the statue of robe-clad figure clutching an infant. This looming marble edifice was erected in 1865, just 16 years after Edgar Allan Poe died nearby, at what's now Church Hospital. But it's not the Dark Bard who's honored here—it's the great Thomas Wildey.

Huh? Thomas who?

Wildey was not a famous statesman, politician, or military figure. He was an Odd Fellow—America's first, and a father figure to some 300,000 Odd Fellows around the world. It was in a Baltimore tavern 180 years ago that Wildey founded what became the Independent Order of Odd Fellows.

The Odd Fellows are a fraternal social/benevolent society, not unlike the Masons, the Moose, and the Elks. They are organized into lodges, and through service to the order, members work their way up through various ranks, from mere member to Grand Sovereign Master. (One notable difference between the Odd Fellows and other fraternal groups: no silly hats.) A plaque at the base of Wildey's monument gravely spells out his Odd descendants' duties: WE COMMAND YOU TO VISIT THE SICK, RELIEVE THE DISTRESSED, BURY THE DEAD, AND EDUCATE THE ORPHAN.

These marching orders resounded with greater relevance back in 1819, when Baltimore was a filthy, hardscrabble town awash in smallpox, yellow fever, and other pestilence. Sick people, orphans, and widows were plentiful. The English-born Wildey had been associated with an Odd Fellows organization back in the old country. Seeking the camaraderie and support that such a group could provide, he set about organizing a U.S. branch. The first meeting was held in the Seven Stars Tavern in the 600 block of Water Street. (The tavern later burned in the 1904 Great Fire.) The first lodge included a mere five Fellows, but the concept quickly took hold in the burgeoning city (and country). By 1831 the lodge had erected an impressive Gothic hall at the corner of Gay and Lexington streets. (The hall was demolished in 1890; two years later, the Odd Fellows built a looming Romanesque temple at Saratoga and Cathedral streets, which now serves as an office building.) The group ultimately severed ties with its English antecedent and, as the Independent Order of Odd Fellows, it began zealously spreading Odd Fellowship around the world. (There are no "Odd Gals," as such. The order remains male-only, but has a sister organization called the Rebekahs.)

One of the most-asked questions of Odd Fellows concerns the group's name. The commonly accepted explanation goes back to the order's working-class origins, according to Robert Beatty, grand secretary of Maryland's Odd Fellows.

"Oh, we get kidded about it," Beatty says. "The name goes back to England and a time when only the nobility formed self-help groups. It was odd for the common people to have such a group so they called them 'odd fellows.'"

By the turn of the century, anyone snickering about the funny name probably didn't do so for long—there were more than a million Odd Fellows nationwide. (The group boasted that every seventh man in Indiana was an Odd Fellow.) But from that zenith, membership has been on the skids (as it has for most fraternal groups). Insurance companies and Social Security have taken on many of the more pragmatic elements of the order's original mission; lifestyle and social changes (not to mention the invention of TV) have altered the way many folks choose to spend their free time.

"The way life is today, people are just too busy working," Beatty says. "Younger people don't seem to have time for us."

There are now about 2,000 Odd Fellows in Maryland, if you also count the Rebekahs. National headquarters moved from Baltimore to North Carolina in the 1970s, but there are 11 local lodges, stretching from Dundalk to Catonsville. While orphanages, formerly one of the order's chief responsibilities (it once ran 80 of them) have fallen out of favor, the Fellows continue to do various charitable works. Nationally, the Odd Fellows contributed $1 million to a research chair at Johns Hopkins' Wilmer Eye Institute; manage dozens of senior-housing centers (including a large assisted-living facility in Frederick); and raise millions of dollars each year for a variety of charities.

The Odd Fellows still get one moment a year in the national spotlight, on New Year's Day, when they sponsor a float in the Rose Parade. But unless it starts attracting new blood, the order—and the name of Thomas Wildey—will slip further into obscurity.

"I'm 47," Beatty remarks, "And I'm considered one of the young ones."

Brennen Jensen
January 20, 1999

Sam the Joke Man

Sam Moss is in his element. We're sharing a booth at Pikesville's Suburban House Restaurant. I'm noshing on a matzo ball the size of a grapefruit. Moss is making people laugh.

"I got a good story to tell you about Monica Lewinksy—did you hear this one?" he starts off. "Monica went to her dry cleaner a couple of weeks ago with a dress under her arm. The man behind the counter, he didn't hear too well and has a huge hearing aid in his ear. He says, 'Can I help you?'

"'Yes,' Monica replies, 'I have a dress here, would you mind taking the stain out of it?'

"'Come again?' the cleaner says, cupping his hand to his ear.

"'No, this time it's mustard.'"

Moss' eyes twinkle mischievously. A broad grin spreads

beneath his silver mustache. He's in his element all right—the affable, white-haired, 81-year-old is telling bawdy jokes, flirting playfully with the waitresses, and greeting old friends.

"Good to see you, Sam," a large man says, stopping by our table. "Remember when we all went to the Colts game in Pittsburgh?"

"Oh, yes, you were just a small boy," Moss replies.

"And remember," the big man continues, "you answered the door for room service in your birthday suit?"

Moss' eyes twinkle even more.

"I like to have fun," he says with a shrug and a smile. "I get so much enjoyment out of life. I do."

As the youngest of nine children growing up in an East Baltimore rowhouse, Moss learned early on that being funny was a way to get noticed. From his immigrant parents he learned the Yiddishisms and old-world accents that mark his stories. And Moss has a lot of stories.

"I'm the only one who knew what my mother was saying," he says. "She spoke in a Yiddish phraseology that only I could understand."

Baltimore's answer to Jackie Mason hit his career peak in the '70s, when he released two comedy albums, *Sam Moss Live* and *Jewish Connection Part 2*. (With routines such as "Urinals" and "The Odorless Toilet" among the cuts, there are traces of Howard Stern in these records.)

Moss says his good friend, erstwhile appliance-store magnate Jack Luskin ("The Cheapest Guy in Town!"), put him up to the recordings. They are full of routines both broad and blue, such as a bit about an Orthodox rabbi's first visit to a cathouse; many of his riffs have fun with Yiddish-tinged mispronunciations, as when Moss describes three ladies debating what material to use in building a new wing of the synagogue. (One suggests "cockrete," another "shitment," and a Mrs. Bloomberg asserts that they should use "pricks," because "pricks stand up!")

Moss never made it to *The Tonight Show* stage or even a Catskills supper club; he had a home-improvement business to run. "I couldn't go into being a comedian professionally," he says. "I had to make a living. I raised three children, and all of them had the finest education in the world." He has no regrets about the road not taken. For 15 years, he did get to broadcast his humor and boundless mirth over the area's radio airwaves. *The Sam Moss Hour of Jewish Comedy and Pride* was a homespun pastiche of music, nostalgia, and fun, featuring movie reviews from "Rex Yid," a segment called "Who's Who in Famous Jews," and, of course, jokes.

"I was like a guy that smokes marijuana," Moss says. "I'd get in front of a microphone and I'd get a lift. I couldn't tell dirty jokes on the radio—but I told some cloudy ones." The show aired on a couple of local stations, most recently WCBM. Judging from the fan mail he received, Moss says, as many non-Jews as Jews were tuning in to the Sunday-morning and -evening shows.

Moss retired from the airwaves two years ago, but he hasn't stopped, only slowed down. Indeed, his sense of humor remains a source of strength. It's what helped him survive his stint in the Army during World War II, when he saw humanity at its worst. And now his disposition helps him keep going in the face of two bum knees and aneurysm surgery.

"I went to meet God a couple of times, but He sent me back," Moss says. "God said I had more comedy to deliver."

By the time my whitefish salad arrives, Moss is back doing his holy duty. "Have you heard the one about the Jewish girls Sadie and Molly?" he asks. "You see, they're both in their late 40s and still virgins and…"

Brennen Jensen
March 24, 1999

Old Money

*O*n a stunningly beautiful Locust Point day, people pass through the door of Hull Federal Savings Bank, a tiny financial institution that has operated out of a rowhouse storefront since 1924. They lean against the plywood counter and do what they've done for decades: Put their affairs in the hands of Wilbur Baumann.

Baumann, 83, is the financial officer for this three-employee bank, which didn't have a telephone until the federal government forced it to update in 1989. Baumann is the institution's soul; his business savvy prevented the bank's closure in 1982 during the savings-and-loan crisis. He is also a Locust Point fixture, known for his stories and his growing canon of organ-music tapes. (He plays the instrument himself.) He tells amazing stories to customers, all day long: How he met movie star Ingrid Bergman while in the army (her autographed picture hangs in his office). How he made bicycle inner tubes out of garden hoses during the Depression. How he's heard that in the early days of World War I, before the United States entered the conflict, a German submarine would sneak through the Allied blockade into the Baltimore harbor and crew members would stop in his father's grocery in Locust Point—which was then populated by German immigrants—to buy bed linen and play music.

As a kid, Baumann says, he tested the existence of God by making a series of wishes that came true—to save his dog from a cut artery, to score the winning goal in a street-hockey game, to attend the World Series. "That's how the Lord set me up," he says.

Tom Sparzak walks into the bank, dirty from a morning haul at a building demolition. He almost gets weepy when he explains how Baumann's bank gave him a loan that saved his house when no other bank would touch him. "I know [Hull Federal] helped a lot of people," he says.

The bank was started in 1911 by Baumann's father's cousin, who used to lend stevedores 50 cents at a time from his plumbing-supply store, which was located next to what is now the Hull Street Blues Café. Thirteen years later, Hull Federal opened up in its current location. Today, it's one of the few remaining neighborhood banks in the city.

With its ceiling fans, oversized pictures of Fort McHenry, Civil War books, and 35-cent fee for issuing money orders, Hull may look a little bit out of step, but it's ready for Y2K, Baumann says.

An Army bookkeeper in World War II and former H&R Block tax accountant and a Johns Hopkins laboratory technician, Baumann knows his customers' account numbers by heart, balances the books by hand, and routinely tests the accuracy of his bank's computer. Not that Baumann has an aversion to technology. He's as apt to click a mouse as he is to bang out a letter on an old manual typewriter. He's amazingly free with numbers; a pamphlet-sized financial statement reveals everything from Hull Federal's total assets ($8.3 million) to the value of its office furniture and supplies ($13,113).

While customers offer testimonies of easy dealings, Baumann says that each transaction is carefully considered. Most of Hull Federal's customers have a history with the bank that goes back two or three generations. For all its down-home appearance, Hull Federal is a conservative lending institution with a rating from the Independent Community Bankers of America that's high enough to attract buyout offers from bigger banks.

"They could buy us out," says Michael Baumann, a bank director. "We could be officers and be wealthy. But we're a community bank. Money doesn't drive us."

Sitting at the computer in the back office, Michael Baumann glances down towards his cousin Wilbur, who is 27 years his senior. Michael worries about Wilbur's stubbornness. Even after two heart attacks, Wilbur Baumann can barely be persuaded to take an aspirin and won't even consider bypass surgery. Wilbur claims the incidents were nothing more than bad cases of heartburn. Such tenacity is probably what saved Hull when the federal government was scrutinizing savings and loans.

"I don't know what was in him, but he fought and fought until he got the federal charter," Michael Baumann says. He recalls with amazement Wilbur's showdown in 1989 with a state board of banking regulators who advised that Hull Federal needed to hire a chief executive officer, then asked how Hull Federal would pay a CEO's salary.

"We could pay him $15,000," Wilbur blasted back, sending the board members into hysterics.

But to Wilbur, it was no joke. He was only paying himself $5,000 per year. Hull did get federal assurance in 1989 after adding two more employees. Wilbur recalls with disdain the days when federal inspectors went over the bank's operations, forbidding such practices as taking the books home. Records had to be kept at the bank, the feds said, and the bank could no longer just be open on Tuesdays from 7 to 9 p.m.—it had to stay open for the entire business week. Since then, Wilbur Baumann has been at the bank office every day, including Saturday and Sundays.

Will he ever retire? "What am I going do, sit around and do nothing?" he asks. "I like to play with figures."

Charles Cohen
April 28, 1999

Postscript: Wilbur Baumann remains a fixture at Hull Federal. With increased development and real-estate activity in Locust Point, the bank continues to attract the interest of larger financial institutions, but so far no suitor has been successful. "We've had a couple of offers, but we haven't taken them," Michael Baumann says.

Lotus Land

Baltimore is routinely celebrated as a place where creative people work and develop in obscurity before finding success somewhere else. It's one of those clichés that is all the more annoying for being true.

Take the case of Gertrude Stein, the oft-cited, little-read materfamilias of modernism. Although Stein's sojourn here predated her career as a writer, Baltimore provided characters and setting for her first published novel, *Three Lives*. Perhaps more importantly, Baltimore gave Stein her first immersion in a community of artists.

Stein was raised in Oakland, California (target of her famous "There's no there there" gibe), but she had strong ties to Baltimore. Her German-born father had immigrated here; her mother was a Mobtown native. As a teenager, before attending Radcliffe College, Stein lived for a while at the home of her uncle, photographer David Bachrach, at 2406 Linden Avenue in Reservoir Hill.

Bachrach's house—still standing, though in pathetic disrepair—was a mecca for Jewish artists and intellectuals. Other relatives lived in Pikesville, and Stein's art-collecting pals, Etta and Claribel Cone (of Baltimore Museum of Art Cone Collection fame), resided at the Marlborough Apartments on Eutaw Place. Stein enjoyed rubbing shoulders with the city's working-class people, and the pace of life here suited her. "Baltimore, sunny Baltimore," she wrote as a Radcliffe student, "where no one is in a hurry and the voices of the negroes singing as their carts go lazily by lull you into drowsy reveries.... The lotus-eaters knew not the joys of calm more completely than a Baltimorean."

After graduating magna cum laude from Radcliffe, Stein moved to Baltimore in 1897 for what would prove to be her longest and most fateful stay in the city.

Her mentor at Radcliffe, famed philosopher William James, advised her to study medicine to round out her psychology degree, and Johns Hopkins University was the logical place to go. Stein's brother, Leo, was already pursuing a biology degree at Hopkins, and it was the school's policy to give female students the same opportunities as males.

As housemates, Gertrude and Leo indulged in a scruffy, bohemian lifestyle. One male relative reminisced, rather fondly, that "[Gertie] went flopping around the place—other girls wore corsets then, but I never liked corsets anyway—big and floppy and sandalled and not caring a damn."

Gertrude's free spirit was not confined to home. Despite the med school's official openness to female students, she ruffled feathers there by "insisting," as one classmate put it, "on seeing and doing things quite unsuitable for a woman."

Although Stein had enough talent to win the support of some professors—including, she later wrote, "the big men like Halsted Osler etcetera"—her frank dislike of obstetrics led her to flunk the course, which prevented her from earning a medical degree. In her autobiography, Stein tells how she actually thanked the professor who failed her for rescuing her from a career that didn't suit her. "The professor was completely taken aback," she wrote, "and that was the end of the medical education of Gertrude Stein."

Shrugging off Hopkins, Gertrude lingered awhile in Baltimore, then followed Leo, who had sailed to Europe after his graduation. Her next long-term address was 27 Rue de Fleurus in Paris, where she collected paintings, boosted Picasso and Matisse, and, as matron of the city's avant-garde, became a celebrity in her own right.

Stein's Baltimore residences are obscure by comparison. Biographers say she lived near the medical school in 1897 and '98, but the city directories for those years have no listings for Gertrude or Leo Stein. Directories for 1899 and 1900 put both Steins at 215 East Biddle Street, a Mount Vernon rowhouse. After Leo sailed for Europe, Gertrude took a place of her own; the 1901 directory lists her at 220 East Eager Street.

In *Three Lives*, Stein offers a description that matches the place on Eager Street: two stories with marble steps and a red-brick face, "a funny little house, one of a whole row of all the same kind that made a close pile like a row of dominoes that a child knocks over, for they were built along a street which at this point came down a steep hill."

The year of Stein's nongraduation was 1901. *Three Lives* appeared nine years later.

Tom Chalkley
June 9, 1999

Beautiful Swimmers

There's a rule for parents on the first day they drop their children off at Marvin Thorpe's backyard swimming pool: Don't hang around. Even if their child is only 3 or 4, frightened and crying, Thorpe insists parents restrain their instincts and walk away.

The prospect might seem more intimidating if Thorpe weren't such an old hand at the swimming-lesson game. But he's been teaching kids to navigate the water for 29 years, and, with his trademark mix of toughness and love, Thorpe knows what he's doing.

As much as it's a local institution, one almost expects Thorpe's backyard to be garnished with Roman columns. The L-shaped pool behind his Woodlawn house is where hundreds of Baltimore-area kids and adults learned to swim.

Thorpe, a retired physical-education teacher who has worked in a slew of city schools, didn't set out to spend his summers teaching people to swim. But in 1970, his 3-year-old

son almost drowned while Thorpe was cleaning his then above-ground swimming pool. The boy was sitting on the edge, dangling his legs, and slipped into the water. Thorpe spotted his son and pulled him out, but he realized what would have happened if he hadn't been there in time. There and then he taught his son the basics, and soon found himself doing the same for neighbors, both young and old.

Aaron Ragsdale, 19, a childhood neighbor and now a swimming instructor himself, was literally handed over the fence to Thorpe for lessons when he was 3. "My father handed me across the fence 'cause I didn't want to come over here," Ragsdale says as he wades chest-high in the water in Thorpe's pool and barks instructions ("Kick! Kick!") at a student nearly three times his age.

Thorpe, a Red Cross-certified swimming instructor (meaning he's passed a lifeguard course that teaches skills such as CPR), presides over a staff of 12 instructors, ranging in age from 14 to 19, who lead three classes a day. Sessions last two weeks, and whether the students are 3 or 50, Thorpe guarantees that when they leave, they'll be swimming.

The immaculate in-ground pool, with its blue tiling and submerged benches, is the centerpiece of this homegrown school, over which Thorpe presides with a persona somewhere between guru and drill sergeant. When children arrive, he tells them crying and whining will not be tolerated. They can't run to their parents because the parents aren't there. And he doesn't need a lifeguard's whistle to get their attention.

"I have to establish rapport with that child," says Thorpe, who is friendly and soft-spoken when he's off duty. "I'm a strong disciplinarian. It's important to learn that you got to respect the water." He warns kids not step near the deep end and to resist the temptation to frolic. He also has to get them to hold their breath underwater—not an easy concept for young minds to grasp. For those who don't believe it's possible, Thorpe puts his hands over their mouth and nose and dunks them.

It's a shocking moment. But when the children realize they can hold their breath, they take to the water like guppies. By the fourth day, when the parents are finally allowed to observe their children, what they see is little swimmers-in-progress. The kids might not be doing the butterfly, but they zip through the pool doing an abbreviated breaststroke, kicking and splashing. "They'll pick up the rest as they go along," says Thorpe, who sends graduates on to other swim clubs for more advanced lessons.

Nicole McCullough was initially concerned about leaving her 3-year-old daughter, Raeden, and 5-year-old son, Eben, at Thorpe's pool. "They say you should teach them when they are young, but I was afraid [they] would get an ear infection," she says. Now, a week and a half later, she is videotaping a smiling Raeden jumping off a diving board and paddling, her face puffed with exertion.

In an odd way, the classes are an exercise in role reversal. Small children swim with confidence. Adults gingerly navigate the waters, thrilled looks on their faces. And teenagers are the law.

One of Thorpe's star teachers, 14-year-old Liana Jenifer, who instructs kids, asks him if it's any different teaching adults. "I don't know," he says. "Let's go find out." He looks out over the pool as Jenifer guides a 50-year-old woman through her maiden voyage into the deep end.

Afterward, Dorothy Vaughan returns to the shallow end to contemplate what she's just done. She's here as a result of a birthday resolution, to do some things for herself.

"I could not swim at all—I was afraid to stick my head under water," she says. But coming to Marvin Thorpe and his staff, she adds, "I know I had people to rescue me."

Charles Cohen
July 28, 1999

The Long Way Home

During his lifetime, Sidney Yellin didn't talk much about the *Hatikvah*. He didn't tell stories about piloting the ship full of Jewish refugees into British-controlled Palestine in 1947, or the months he spent in a refugee camp in Cyprus as a result, or the medal he was awarded by Israel for his role in its founding.

"He didn't even talk to his children about it," his widow, Judith Yellin, says. "I would keep bringing it up 'cause I wanted them to know about it, but it was like pulling teeth."

Sidney Yellin died in February at the age of 77, of complications from diabetes. Since then, Judith Yellin has made it her mission to talk about the things her husband kept to himself. She believes he deserves some notoriety, perhaps even a movie or TV miniseries about his adventure on the converted ice-cutter *Hatikvah*. Then a captain in the merchant marine, he agreed at the urging of a Baltimore-based Zionist group to take the assignment, knowing the ship would almost certainly be intercepted by British forces trying to stop the post-World War II flow of Jews who were defiantly trying to settle in Palestine.

There's no trace of bitterness or sadness in Judith Yellin's voice as she wraps herself up in her husband's story. Sitting in the office of her electrolysis business, located above a pharmacy in Pikesville, she displays photos of Sidney and the David Ben-Gurion Centennial Medal he was awarded by Israel in 1987. The medal was accompanied by a proclamation: "We recollect not only the horrors of the Diaspora's Holocaust, we remember also those wonderful people who stretched out their hands and divided the sea for us, who gave us hope."

It's not the memorabilia but the telling of the story that puts Judith Yellin's memories of her husband in motion. She smiles when she recalls him as a "toughie—as short [5-foot-7] as he was, he was tough." He spent his childhood in Baltimore orphanages and foster homes and hopped trains with hobos before running away at age 16 to join the merchant marine in 1937.

"He was one of the few Jews in the fleet," Judith says. "Every time he went on the ship for the first time he had to fight and show [his shipmates] that he could stand up to them, and he did." During World War II he rose to the rank of captain, piloting freighters in dangerous convoys that were vulnerable to attack.

In early 1947, back home in Baltimore between assignments, Sidney Yellin was approached by a group of local Jewish leaders who were trying to help the thousands of Jews go to Palestine. It was a volatile time for Jewish survivors of Hitler's concentration camps; many were in refugee camps throughout Europe, stranded by Western nations' strict quotas on Jewish immigration. Those who'd escaped to Palestine were embroiled in a violent struggle for statehood, fighting not just Arabs but the British, the League of Nations-appointed guardians of Palestine. The Baltimore group had a boat rigged with extra bunks to carry more than 1,400 people; they needed a captain and a crew of 30 to try to run the

British blockade, designed to keep Jews from going to Palestine.

After a day's contemplation, Yellin agreed to serve as captain. Judith Yellin says her husband was a passionate believer in the Israeli cause, but Anita Kassof—who interviewed him while curating *Bridges to Zion*, a 1998 Jewish Museum of Maryland exhibit about local involvement in the founding of Israel—says he wasn't entirely motivated by Zionism: "I think this was another adventure for him, and it was only in hindsight [that] this had greater meaning."

The plan was for the ship to get captured by the British; the refugees expected to end up in a camp in Cyprus and await the formation of Israel, which they believed was imminent.

In February 1947, under cover of darkness, two ships, dubbed the *Hatikvah* and the *Exodus*, left Baltimore for Italy, where they would pick up their human cargo. A storm forced the less-seaworthy *Exodus* to turn back to Norfolk, Virginia, according to Joseph M. Hochstein and Murray S. Greenfield's book *The Jews' Secret Fleet*, but the *Hatikvah* continued on. It docked in Lisbon for several weeks for more renovations, then sailed to the Italian coast to rendezvous with refugees waiting on rubber rafts.

On May 17, as expected, a British destroyer intercepted the refugee ship. It was towed to Haifa, in what is now Israel. As they'd been instructed, the refugees never identified Yellin as the ship's captain. (At times, decoy officers were posted on the ship, including a young boy who did time as "captain.") The refugees, and the crew, were sent to Cyprus.

While the *Hatikvah* passengers were interred, the *Exodus* attempted another crossing. This time the ship made it to the blockade, and engaged the British in a fight in which three Jews were killed. The British captured the ship and sent its 4,500 passengers to refugee camps in France.

In the meantime, the British sent a prison ship to Cyprus to take a small group of the *Hatikvah* refugees to Palestine, where they were going to be allowed to settle. The Americans were to go to Palestine as well, and from there, return to the States. Emboldened by the *Exodus* battle, Hochstein and Greenfield write, the *Hatikvah* crew decided to try and destroy the prison ship. Sidney Yellin and his men coordinated with members of the Jewish underground in Cyprus to smuggle a bomb on board. Once everyone was safely disembarked at Haifa, the bomb went off and the ship sank.

Knowing the British would interrogate them, Sidney Yellin instructed his shipmates to give ridiculous answers rather than try to stick to a prefabricated story. Judith Yellin says he learned the trick—designed to spare prisoners the stress of trying to keep stories straight—as a merchant marine, serving on ships that often faced possible capture during the war. The ploy worked, and the British did not discover who was responsible for the bombing.

Yellin was released by the British and returned to Baltimore in late summer of 1947, to the cheers of the local Jewish community. "I thought he was a big hero from the day I met him," Judith Yellin says. They met not long after his return, at a party; she was 17, he 25. "That's what really attracted me to him. I thought it was a very heroic thing to do, knowing that you were going to be put in a camp." They married three years later.

The journey of the *Exodus* made international news and incited worldwide support for the founding of Israel. The best-selling Leon Uris novel and hit movie starring Paul Newman that it inspired ensured that the *Exodus* would become synonymous with the Jewish statehood struggle. The story of the *Hatikvah*, by contrast, faded into obscurity. (Most local write-ups about the *Exodus* from the period don't even mention the other ship.) Sidney Yellin left the merchant marine and started a successful construction firm; Judith built up her electrolysis business.

It never bothered Sidney that the other ship that briefly sailed alongside his that night in 1947 came to represent this period of pre-Israel history, but it bothers his wife. After her husband's death, she wrote a brief history of his life titled "The Forgotten Hero: Sidney Yellin," which she has sent to Hollywood megadirectors Steven Spielberg and Barry Levinson.

"I'm going to do my damnedest," she says, "to see that his worth comes out."

Charles Cohen
October 27, 1999

Postscript: Judith Yellin is still trying to interest film and television people in her husband's story. A neighbor of the family is working on a screenplay about Sidney Yellin and the Hatikvah.

Soul Sister

Elizabeth Lange was a native of Saint-Domingue—present-day Haiti—whose family fled to Cuba after the 1800 slave revolt led by Toussaint L'Ouverture. Being wealthy Creoles—people of mixed race—she and her family were no longer welcome in their homeland. Perhaps they felt uncomfortable in Cuba too. For whatever reason, many Creoles, including Lange, decided to move to Baltimore in about 1812.

"Why Baltimore? Why would a black woman come to a slave state?" Sister Virginie Fish lets the question sink in for a moment. "All things happen by God's intent," she explains. A retired teacher, Sister Virginie is a member of the Oblate Sisters of Providence, the small, mainly African-American order of nuns that Elizabeth Lange—better known as Mother Lange—founded in Baltimore in 1829.

Today, Mother Lange's followers want her to be recognized as a Roman Catholic saint. If their canonization campaign succeeds, she will be the first African-American saint from outside Latin America. Sister Virginie serves as the effort's vice postulator—that is, as assistant to the priest who oversees research and promotional efforts on Mother Lange's behalf.

Most of Lange's saintly work was carried out at St. Frances Academy, now located at 501 East Chase Street and still run by the Oblate Sisters. Officially, the school traces its beginnings to 1828—one year before the Oblate Sisters were organized—but its origins go back still farther.

Baltimore in the early 1800s had a large free-black population, but white schools and teachers generally refused to teach children of color, including Creole refugees. Recognizing a desperate need, Lange, then a lay person, established a school in her house on Bank Street in Fells Point. She ran the school for a decade, drawing on her own inheritance for funding. Meanwhile, on the west side of town, a French-born priest, the Rev. James Hector Joubert, was trying—and failing—to persuade white nuns to take black students. Frustrated, Joubert appealed to Archbishop James Whitfield to create an order of African-American nuns to do the job, and invited Lange and two other Haitian-born teachers to be its first adherents. On July 2, 1829, the three made vows of poverty, chastity, and obedience, and took on the title of "Oblate," which means (in Sister Virginie's words) "to make an offering of your life to God." Lange was renamed Sister Mary. In recognition of her leadership skills, she was chosen to be the "superior" of the group.

Much of Mother Lange's legend stems from her lifelong struggle to carry out her mission despite the pervasive racism of her time. In their first months, the Oblates and their school were shunted from one set of cramped quarters to another in the Seton Hill area before finding a house on Richmond Street, not far from the modern intersection of Park Avenue and Read Street. After the death of Joubert and Whitfield, the Oblates fell on hard times; the new archbishop, Samuel Eccleston, saw no purpose in teaching black children and suggested that the nuns disband and find menial jobs. To survive, Mother Lange and her followers became housekeepers and cooks for white clergy at St. Mary's Seminary (then located downtown) and elsewhere. They scrupulously managed their meager pay to keep their school intact. In 1870, the school moved to its present location, where it continues to this day to struggle against the social legacy of institutional racism.

The only known photograph of Mother Lange is a fuzzy image from her old age, showing a dark-skinned woman with high cheekbones and penetrating eyes. Posthumous portraits of the prospective saint are essentially "age regressions" based on this one picture. She died in 1882 in a room at St. Frances.

Ten years ago, Mother Lange's admirers took the first steps toward her canonization. The process involves a series of rigorous investigations and tests of the nominee's life and works, including a study of putative miracles attributable to her intercession with the Almighty. Sister Virginie distributes petitions, lectures to all who will listen, and sells books, pamphlets, plaques, and coloring books about Mother Lange to support the cause.

"People ask, 'Why? What difference does it make [if Mother Lange is canonized]?'" Again, Sister Virginie lets the question sink in. "Why do we have the Nobel Prize? Why do we have the Olympics? Why do we have public monuments? Because it serves as a stimulus, an impetus, an example." And, I might note, it can't hurt Baltimore to have a friend in heaven.

Tom Chalkley
December 1, 1999

Postscript: On February 13, 2000, the City of Baltimore honored Mother Mary Lange and the Oblate Sisters with a ceremony recognizing the order's 171 years of service to city residents. A bronze marker was placed at 610 George Street in Seton Hill, site of the order's first school. Subsequently, a delegation of Oblate Sisters made a pilgrimage to Rome, where they presented Pope John Paul II with materials about Mother Lange, and met with Roman Catholic officials about their sanctification campaign.

Charmed Places

Bones but No Bonapartes

Fifteen years ago, when I started doing business at the Waverly Post Office, I noticed some grim-looking stucco walls nearby and assumed they belonged to the Coldstream Park Recreation Center next-door. The walls are 8 feet tall and surmounted by two rows of iron spikes, which tend to discourage prying eyes. Years passed before I took the trouble to peek inside.

On the south wall I found an iron gate, locked and topped with more spiky grillwork, and an oval plate bearing the date 1793. Using the lock as a foothold, I clambered up, clung to the spikes, and peered through the grille. Inside was a rectangular yard some 60 feet by 40 feet, buried in dead leaves; lining the

walls was a series of severe, algae-green grave markers and coffinlike tombs. Several mature oaks stood over the graves.

The spiky walls have served their builders well; only a few soda bottles desecrate the cemetery. But outside there's faded graffiti by BIG WORM, LI'L TIFF, and others. The stucco has been torn off in places, exposing old bricks; a pile of construction trash—possibly from the rehab project going on across Fillmore Street from the graveyard—slumps against the wall beside the gate. It's clear no one takes care of the place.

This neglected plot shelters the remains of one of Baltimore's early titans, the shipping baron William Patterson (1752-1835). An immigrant from Northern Ireland, Patterson came to Baltimore in 1778 and pursued a career of heroic entrepreneurship. At great risk he imported French ammunition for George Washington's army; he fought at Yorktown; he was a founder of the B&O Railroad; he donated the land that became Patterson Park. He also owned a heap of real estate, including the cemetery site. It occupies a high point of land that, two centuries ago, must have offered mourners a suitably idyllic view.

In his will, a rambling text that includes a sort of confessional memoir, Patterson called for a monument "with four or six sides" to stand over his grave and that of his wife, Dorcas Spear Patterson, who died in 1814. In all, historians say, 20 or 22 of William's descendants and relatives share the graveyard. The last interred was his granddaughter Laura, who died in 1918 at the age of 94.

Two Patterson descendants are conspicuous by their absence. One is William's daughter Elizabeth, remembered today as Betsy Patterson Bonaparte because she married Napoleon Bonaparte's younger brother Jerome. This union displeased Napoleon, who—being one of history's great social climbers—insisted his sibling pick a bride from a royal family. The French emperor ordered his brother back to Europe—presumably on threat of disinheritance—and unilaterally annulled the marriage. Jerome became king of Westphalia; Betsy, who had borne a son named

Jerome Napoleon Bonaparte, was paid off with a pension. The junior Jerome is buried in West Baltimore's Loudon Park Cemetery, and Betsy is one of Green Mount Cemetery's celebrity tenants.

Betsy's exclusion from the family plot isn't surprising. She was largely disinherited by her father, who complained in his will that she caused him "more anxiety and trouble than all my other children put together." She also scorned her Baltimore roots, and retired here only after wearing out her welcome in European society.

Historical fact notwithstanding, neighborhood folks called the old graveyard the "Bonaparte cemetery" as recently as the 1960s. Back then, according to Waverly native and raconteur Charlie Doble, prankish teenagers would get younger kids buzzed on beer and persuade them to go over the walls, either with a ladder or via overhanging tree limbs. Once inside they were trapped, and the teens wouldn't tip a ladder over the spikes until their victims were driven to tears. Doble underwent such a hazing one mid-'60s autumn night, but—as he tells it—he refused to give his tormentors the satisfaction of hearing him cry. The hour grew late, the night got cold, his captors got bored, the ladder came over, and Doble lived to tell the tale.

Tom Chalkley
January 7, 1998

Far East Baltimore

*N*ew York has one. So does San Francisco. There's one just an hour away in Washington. But Baltimore doesn't have one. Not anymore.

Stroll along the 300 block of Park Avenue and you'll find

crumbling rowhouses festooned with faded Chinese characters, boarded-up Chinese restaurants (the White Rice Inn's battered exterior advertises FAMOUS CHINESE FAMILY DINNERS), and signs for a Chinese Free Mason Lodge and a Chinese Merchant Association on dark, padlocked buildings that infer—well, proclaim—a lack of recent activity.

Baltimore is proud of its neighborhoods and ethnic enclaves—from storied Little Italy to burgeoning Spanish Town. But our Chinatown is pretty much a ghost town.

"Baltimore's Chinatown was always small because there never were very many Chinese here," says Lillian Kim, the 78-year-old matriarch of the city's Chinese community and author of a history chronicling Baltimore's early Chinese families. The first of her countrymen, she says, came here around 1865. (And they were all, at first, countrymen; harsh U.S. laws—including a "Chinese Exclusion Act"—severely limited immigration from China, making it difficult for male pioneers to send for their wives.)

The city's first Chinese enclave formed around Marion Street (today an alley running behind the Fayette Street Greyhound bus terminal). The famed Chinese politician Sun Yat-sen lived here in 1902 while soliciting funds from Chinese in the United States for his revolutionary activities back home. By the 1920s Baltimore's Chinese residents—numbering only a few hundred—had moved their noodle factories, groceries, restaurants, and hand laundries to the blocks around the intersection of Park Avenue and Mulberry Street. On-Leong, a merchants' association that helped Chinese entrepreneurs (and enforced a set of self-imposed regulations, such as one that kept competing laundries at least 1,000 feet apart), relocated there as well. Chinatown became the center of the Chinese community's economic and cultural—if not domestic—activity.

"Baltimore is kind of unusual in that there were never many people living in Chinatown," says Kim, who grew up around Hollins Market after arriving here as a child in 1921. "We lived all over the city."

Ironically, while World War II ravaged much of China, with that country a U.S. ally against Japan the conflict greatly improved the lives of Baltimore's Chinese, loosening immigration restrictions and fostering greater acceptance and employment opportunities. (A high percentage of Baltimore's Chinese served in the U.S. armed forces.) A new generation of Chinese-Americans was emerging, it seemed—one less bound by Old World tradition and New World prejudice. And by the 1950s newspaper articles were reporting the demise of Chinatown.

Twenty years ago a last-ditch effort to revitalize Chinatown was launched. A group of Chinese-American merchants ambitiously planned a $20 million Asian Cultural Center, with a 10-story office/apartment/shopping complex and a giant "peace pagoda." But the funds were never raised.

Now, Chinese stir-fry is sold from Glen Burnie to Bel Air,

and Baltimore's Chinatown is quiet. But amid the shuttered shops, one mom-and-pop grocery remains: a jumbled, narrow store called Potung Trading, which offers salted duck eggs, dried lotus seeds, and bushelbaskets of gnarled ginger root (alongside beepers, videos, and compact discs). The taciturn proprietor says he doesn't know anything about Chinatown's history or decline; he's only owned the store a short while. But his younger colleague is as concise as a fortune cookie.

"Everyone," he says, "has moved to the suburbs."

Brennen Jensen
January 14, 1998

Shop Talk

"If you are tired of shopping," Wallis Warfield Simpson, the Baltimore-reared Duchess of Windsor, once remarked, "you are going to the wrong shops."

These days the "right shops"—judging by the tireless, happy throngs that fill them—are at The Avenue in White Marsh. It's the oldfangled new face of shopping—a slick re-creation of an old-time Main Street that debuted last fall. The buildings housing the (mostly chain) stores along The Avenue's length are designed to mimic what might have been seen in mythical Mayberry. (There's a firehouse, a hardware store, a mill, and so forth.) It's all in the shadow of the Rouse Company's massive White Marsh Mall, but this, it seems, is of little concern.

"Indoor shopping malls are boring," an urban designer said in an article in *The Sun* about The Avenue's opening. "It's new to be outside, to see fresh air."

The changing shape of consumption is a curious affair. But as a quick tour of the region reveals, it's nothing new to

Baltimore. We've been at the forefront of shopping-center evolution for more than a century.

Travel about 10 miles west-southwest from White Marsh (the suburbs of the 1990s) to Roland Park (the suburbs of the 1890s). Tucked in this leafy enclave, the sweeping streets of which where laid out partly by landscape architect Frederick Olmstead Jr. (son of the famed designer of New York's Central Park), is the country's first shopping center. Built in 1896 along the 4800 block of Roland Avenue, the trim, handsome Roland Park Shopping Center sports stores on the first floor with offices above. The design motif is Old English: half-timbered gables, diamond-paned windows, dormers poking from a steeply pitched roof.

The International Council of Shopping Centers places the nation's first shopping center in Missouri in 1922, and the book *The Malling of America* says the first one was in Illinois in 1916. But a metal sign mounted in front of the still-thriving Roland Park center—bearing the stalwart imprimatur of the National Register of Historic Places—confirms its exalted status. The 19th-century building, the sign declares, "pioneered the concept of shopping centers in the United States."

But being historic is not enough: In the mid-'70s a developer nearly razed the landmark structure, wanting to replace it with a modern shopping center. Wiser heads prevailed, and the building was left unmolested.

Some 15 miles due south of Roland Park is Harundale, the suburbs of the 1940s. Amid this meandering collection of humble, slab-foundation ranch houses is the first enclosed shopping mall east of the Mississippi (and the first mall built by a single developer, in this case the Rouse Company). Harundale Mall opened with festive fanfare in 1958, just two years after the nation's first mall debuted in Edina, Minnesota. Sen. John F. Kennedy, pressing the flesh in preparation for the presidential-campaign trail, dropped by to cut the ribbon. Inside shoppers found fanciful flourishes such as caged myna birds and tropical gardens. Exotica aside, the mall was designed, according to news reports at the time, along the lines of an "old-time market square."

Rouse had cut its teeth in the shopping-center biz two years earlier, building the Mondawmin Shopping Center on the city's west side. (By the '60s Mondawmin and many other early shopping centers—Westview, Reisterstown Plaza, and Eastpoint, to name a few—had followed the Harundale lead and were roofed over into malls to meet public preference for climate-controlled consumerism.) Rouse grew into a shopping-mall juggernaut, spreading Muzak-filled temples of consumption across the land. And in the '70s Rouse conceived the "urban festival marketplace," the most famous—and copied—version being our own Harborplace.

But again, being historic is not enough: Harundale Mall, Rouse's first goldmine, has been closed for several months now, save for a Value City department store housed in a former Hochshild Kohn. The mall is slated to be razed. The myna birds are long gone, as are the shoppers—they've been lured to greener pastures in which to spend their green.

Which brings us full circle to The Avenue, some 15 miles northeast of Harundale. Hour-long waits are not unusual at Avenue eateries; showings at its looming 16-screen movie theater often sell out. This is where the action is. For now.

And if The Avenue's panache should fade in the future? Well, they could always build a roof over it.

Brennen Jensen
February 4, 1998

Small Town

Druid Hill Park contains many strange and wonderful things. One of them is Baltimore's Model Safety City. Just how strange or wonderful it is depends on your point of view.

Back in my nonparent days, Safety City was a regular stop on the surreal Balto-Tours I gave to guests and newcomers. We'd loop into the park via the Druid Lake entrance, pass the ferocious statue of 13th-century Scottish patriot William Wallace, turn right after the Columbus monument, and find Safety City wedged between a tennis court and a cemetery that predates the park. The sign in those days read simply BALTIMORE'S MODEL SAFETY CITY, with none of the further explanation provided by the metal placard in place today.

If you've never seen it, picture this: a fenced enclosure, roughly the size of a baseball diamond, with well-marked asphalt streets, cement sidewalks, and a collection of miniature buildings, most lacking any semblance of doors or windows. There are several blocks of tiny, windowless brick rowhouses, a factory with mock skylights and a smokestack, a tin-roofed schoolhouse, a garage, and, most prominent, a 14-foot model of what was once called the USF&G Building. On the north side is an avenue of windowless cottages representing suburbia.

These miniature structures are juxtaposed with specimens of real-world street infrastructure—some scaled down, some not. The traffic signals, which really work, hang low enough for an adult to touch; a genuine city streetlight hovers a mere eight feet over its corner, while the parking meters stand taller than the rowhouses. There is a short section of railroad track; it goes nowhere. The overall effect is something like a gigantic model train setup cobbled together from kits of various gauges. In winter, when Safety City is vacant, the empty streets and faceless structures have a haunted quality that is compounded by the random sense of scale. Gertrude Stein's dictum applies:

There is no there there.

The intent of Safety City's creators was just the opposite of surrealism. According to Fred Shoken, the Department of Public Works employee who oversees the Safety City program, the site was "designed to have all the traffic conditions of a real city" in order to give city children vivid lessons in pedestrian and bicycle safety. Between April and October each year, some 7,000 children attend one-hour training sessions led by former crossing guards. Most of the students are in elementary school—the age group Shoken says suffers the highest rate of pedestrian accidents. They are drawn from schools, Scout groups, and day-care centers throughout the metropolitan area. After their lessons in looking both ways, obeying signals, and not fooling with fire hydrants, the kids get to cruise the streets in battery-powered "Powerwheels"—sporty yellow electric buggies.

The present Safety City was erected in 1986 to replace two earlier layouts created by the Baltimore Police Department's Traffic Safety Education Unit in 1970. The original Safety Cities (one on this site and one behind the Southeastern District police station) featured cozy-looking mini-bungalows built, according to police newsletters, by "local teenagers." Kids rode pedal-powered four-wheelers instead of today's buggies. Assuming they heeded their safety lessons, the earliest graduates of Safety City are now in their late 30s.

By 1985 both of the old sites had deteriorated badly. Several city agencies collaborated on a miniature urban-renewal proposal that got a "do it now" from then-Mayor William Donald Schaefer. City planner Jim Hall was the project's architect. "I remember the emotions," Hall says. "It was a really serious effort to prevent accidents. If we kept a couple little kids from being run over, it was worth it."

Hall's blueprint shows what is not obvious at ground level: Safety City is laid out to fit Baltimore's familiar quadrangular boundaries, with a "harbor" of blue-painted tarmac. The bricks around Safety City's flagpole form a tiny replica of Fort McHenry.

Grown-ups wishing to learn more about the Safety City program should call (410) 396-6655 between April and October. But surrealists should note that my old tour route has been blocked off. I suggest going to the park and wandering aimlessly until you happen upon it.

Tom Chalkley
February 18, 1998

Aquatecture

If you had to choose a structure to serve as Baltimore's architectural testimonial to bricks and mortar, what would it be? The Flag House? The Shot Tower? The Camden Yards warehouse? The new football stadium, where the builders insisted on a pricey brick facade rather than the usual shiny steel?

Fine examples all, perhaps. But if there's one building that truly captures this city's love affair with brick, it's the Curtis Bay Water Tank. Perched on the hill overlooking Curtis Bay and the Patapsco River, the 60-foot tall, 120-foot wide tank is both opulent and obscure. While most water tanks hew to the standard model—metal casing, thin base, distended globular head—the Curtis Bay tank at Prudence and Filbert streets stands as a lost architectural ambassador from a time when even the most mundane municipal structures were conceived with an eye to aesthetics.

Curtis Bay could have been stuck with a squat steel tank, which is exactly what the city built in 1930 to replace a previous water-storage vessel. But in the next couple of years, the city—at the tail end of an era when architectural care was lavished even on public-works facilities (witness the whimsical sewage-pumping

station at President Street and Eastern Avenue or the ornate Montebello Filtration Plant in North Baltimore)—encased the tank in a lavish brick facade.

Principally designed by city engineer Frank Heyder, a specialist in water-supply structures, the 2-foot-thick shell is ringed with classical-looking pilasters and arches, rising to a cross-hatched cornice. It employs more than 20 hues of brick that, arrayed in order from dark to light or light to dark in various parts of the tank, give the illusion of illumination. It must have made for quite a construction job. "I can picture those workers holding those bricks up to the light, trying to figure out which ones were lighter," Baltimore architect Walter Schamu observes. A 1937 *Sun* article reported that the tank "has been called by some the most beautiful piece of brickwork in the nation."

Gazing at the top of the Jefferson Memorial-shaped edifice, Bruce Kenny of Datanet Engineering, a Woodlawn consulting firm, wonders if such a thing could be reproduced today. "I know some bricklayers today would disagree with me," he says, "but I don't think you could find the craftsmanship."

"I can't imagine doing it today," says Schamu, founder of the Historic Architects Round Table (or as members call it, the "Dead Architects Society"), an organization that investigates older buildings in Baltimore, trying to identify which buildings were designed by which architects. "It would be prohibitively expensive, or they'd think that you're crazy, or maybe both."

According to John Dorsey and James D. Dilts' *A Guide to Baltimore Architecture*, Heyder, who died in 1973, had a library of 3,500 books on architecture and was fascinated by cathedrals and domes. That influence manifested itself in his design for the tank, which seems more like a temple than a municipal facility. (Dorsey and Dilts report that it is sometimes mistaken for a synagogue.) Maybe that's the point—water, the source of life, the necessity we probably take most for granted, should be considered holy.

"It's always a bit of a mystery, and kids are always coming up to me and asking what's in there," says Duane Tressler, a Curtis Bay native and local-history buff. He's lobbying the Curtis Bay Community Association to adopt the tank's image to represent the neighborhood on T-shirts and stationery. Tressler's favorite view of the tank is from the Francis Scott Key Bridge. In his eyes, it's as prominent a part of the Baltimore skyline as the downtown office towers and Dundalk's cranes. "I've heard," Tressler says, "that it's the first thing that foreign ships see as soon as they come in."

Charles Cohen
May 6, 1998

Written in Stone

One of the most important—and probably the biggest—of the historic "firsts" Baltimore claims is all but hidden from public view, straddling a wooded stretch of Gwynns Falls on railroad tracks 1.6 miles west of the B&O Railroad Museum. It is the Carrollton Viaduct, constructed in 1829 and the first stone railroad bridge built in the United States. And according to John W. Duvall, writing in the September 1989 issue of *Baltimore Engineer*, the magazine of the Engineering Society of Baltimore, the viaduct has the more remarkable distinction of being the oldest railroad bridge on the entire planet that is still in use.

I've seen pictures of the Carrollton Viaduct for years—one

on a piece of blue-and-white B&O dining-car china—but I never beheld the thing itself until I went hunting for it last month. Acting on a tip, I caught a glimpse of it off to my right from southbound Interstate 95, just before the Caton Avenue exit. Not a safe maneuver at freeway speeds nor, at this time of year, a very satisfying one: The bridge is barely visible behind dense foliage.

For a better look at this landmark, the easiest approach is by way of an access road that parallels Gwynns Falls on the western edge of the Carroll Park Municipal Golf Course. The lane ends abruptly at a heap of yard waste; you must continue on foot, follow a golf-cart road a ways, then plunge into a jungle of 10-foot-high weeds laced with litter-strewn footpaths. The bridge can be seen from the edge of the stream, its main arch hovering some 52 feet over a broad, slow-moving section of the water. Climb up the steep embankment and you'll find that the broad bridge now carries a single track instead of its original two, plus two wooden walkways cantilevered off of the sides. A constant, grating roar heard from the bottom of the bridge turns out not to be the sound of a passing train but the din of the David J. Joseph and Company's scrap-grinding complex on the other side of the tracks.

There's no historic marker to be found anywhere near the viaduct—not surprising, considering its inaccessibility. The following, however, are a few marker-worthy facts, culled from various chronicles of the Baltimore & Ohio Railroad: The viaduct is named for Charles Carroll of Carrollton, signer of the Declaration of Independence, who laid the first stone of the B&O on July 4, 1828; the bridge's construction followed a debate among B&O directors over whether to build it with durable stone or much less expensive wood; one of the military engineers who successfully lobbied for stone was Lt. George Whistler, father of the famous painter (and thus husband of Whistler's mother); the architect on the project was Caspar Wever (spellings of his name vary); the engineer in charge was James Lloyd; age-stained and unspectacular today, it was hailed by one 1830 traveler as a work of "solidity, beauty, and even grandeur."

Construction took more than nine months and 11,000 or 12,000 blocks of granite, most of which came from a quarry near present-day Ellicott City. Huge wooden frameworks were built to support some 1,500 tons of granite until keystones were put in place and the massive arch became self-supporting. The entire structure, now largely obscured by greenery, is roughly 300 feet long and 60 feet tall, with an arch 80 feet wide crossing the stream and a much smaller arch on the west bank, originally used for a wagon road and now conveying a sewer line.

A few more "firsts" are associated with the viaduct. On New Year's Day, 1830, it became America's first railroad destination. In an effort to drum up interest in their fledgling enterprise, the B&O's directors sold one-way tickets to the viaduct—then the end of the line—for 9 cents, or three tickets for a quarter. These paltry sums were the American railroad industry's first revenues. One of the first riders was Alexander Brown, the banker whose namesake investment house was recently engulfed by Banker's Trust.

Those first rail excursions, incidentally, were hauled by horses. The first locomotive, Peter Cooper's "Tom Thumb," crossed the viaduct later in 1830. Trains have used it ever since.

Tom Chalkley
June 3, 1998

Top This

While orbiting the moon in 1969, Apollo astronaut Russell Schweickart held his hand before a window and blocked out the image of his home planet. He later spoke of feeling not godlike, but incredibly tiny.

For a similar sensation you can sit at a table in the Pleasant View Towers Restaurant in Hampden and fit downtown Baltimore between your thumb and forefinger.

The restaurant, on the top floor of the Roland View Towers apartment building at 3838 Roland Avenue, has from time to time promoted itself as the highest vantage point in Baltimore City. Add the words "open to the public" and it's a more accurate—if less ringing—declaration. According to building manager Art Ruby, Roland View Towers rises 150 feet over Roland Avenue on a spot 307 feet above sea level, putting the restaurant's view some 450 feet up. The World Trade Center, by comparison, stands 423 feet above the water, with its Top o' the World observation deck on the building's second-highest floor. Granted, the World Trade Center's view—straight down to the paddleboats and out to the bay—is dizzying and dazzling. The Pleasant View's view is, well, extremely pleasant, and it comes with breakfast, lunch, or dinner.

The restaurant primarily caters to the building's elderly tenants. Nonresidents must sign in at the tower's front desk and press the elevator's "R" button (for "restaurant"). On "R" level, just outside of the elevator, there's a window looking west toward TV Hill. For media snobs this offers a great opportunity to look down, literally, on four of Baltimore's television stations. The wooded hill rises well above WBAL's aeries; at the top are apartments with sightlines that must be even better than Pleasant View's. But enough of such rivalries.

Inside the restaurant, window walls face south, east and north, surveying a panorama of some 270 degrees. The view to the north is mostly trees and rooftops, punctuated by the spire of the Cathedral of Mary Our Queen. To the east are the clustered high-rise apartments at Charles Street and University Parkway and the cupolas of Johns Hopkins University; farther off stand the tower of City College High School and, still farther, the Back River sewage-treatment plant, with twin golden domes that evoke images of Gaultier-clad Madonna.

Facing south, the Key Bridge is completely visible; beyond it are the Sparrows Point steel complex and the lone smokestack of the Brandon Shores Power Plant in Anne Arundel County. Along the horizon lies a sliver of the Eastern Shore.

The downtown skyline is quite handsome from Pleasant View Towers. Instead of silly Inner Harbor confections, you see the Belvedere, City Hall, Commerce Place, the World Trade Center, and the tower that to this writer will always be the Maryland National Building. Now the Bank of America Building, it appears to be higher than the restaurant's lookout, but it isn't open for lunch.

For an even better look around, borrow waitress Barbara Keene's binoculars. She is happy to share the powerful pair with guests.

Far from taking their lofty position for granted, restaurant owner Shirley Harrison and her staff—which includes her daughter, Sherrie—are enthusiastic about it. "What I like best," Sherrie Harrison says, "is that the city looks so different. It looks clean, it looks safe, like nothing bad could happen. Down on street level," she sighs, "it's another story."

After closing time, Shirley Harrison likes to relax on the roof with a snack, but insurance costs prohibit alfresco dining by restaurant patrons. In summer months the restaurant's glittering nightscape is also off limits because the restaurant closes at 8 p.m. (7 p.m. on Sundays).

In addition to the earthbound scenery, the Harrisons tell of celestial events and spectacular atmospherics: sunrises, sunsets, lightning dancing on the railings outside, crystalline views of the Hale-Bopp comet and last winter's planetary alignment. And once, Harrison says, everyone in the place rushed to the window to see a double rainbow straddling the metropolis.

Tom Chalkley
July 15, 1998

Old Alma Mater

When a colleague suggested a visit to the ruins of the Patapsco Female Institute, I pictured something like the horrific girls' school in *Jane Eyre* reduced to a pile of gothic rubble and overgrown with poison ivy. Fifteen years ago I would have been close to the mark—but times have changed.

Perched on a bluff above old Ellicott City, the institute is a safe, sunny, user-friendly ruin, so gloom-free that four weddings have been held there since 1995, when the restored site was opened to the public.

Architecturally it's an anomaly: 1835 classicism reconstructed with the materials and sensibilities of 1995. The original mansard roof has vanished, leaving the whole place open to the sky. On the front porch four stout Tuscan columns exert themselves against thin air. Monumental walls of hand-sawed granite have been sandblasted and reinforced with smooth concrete and blue steel girders. Rot-resistant wooden decks and stylish brick courtyards have replaced floors that were

demolished 40 years ago.

This "stabilization project," as it is modestly termed, was designed by architects Alfonso Narvez and F. Neale Quenzel of John Milner Associates. It's functional yet quietly handsome—much like the original unadorned Greek-revival building designed by Baltimore's Robert Cary Long Jr.

Long's clients were pious investors who wanted a "chaste" yet imposing building suitable for an upper-crust girls' school. The Patapsco Female Institute opened in 1837, its mission (according to the prospectus) "to provide for the daughters of the South facilities for an Education that shall leave nothing to be desired." Patrician daughters, alongside a few "poor girls" on scholarship, were schooled in English, literature, modern and classical languages, "natural and abstract sciences," and fine arts. The institute's most famous alumna was Winny Davis, daughter of Confederate President Jefferson Davis. Although the Civil War took a toll on the school, it struggled on, finally closing its doors in 1891.

Since then the building has lived just about nine lives. In the 1890s it was remodled as a summer hotel. In 1905 it became the home of Lily Tyson Elliott, a descendant of Ellicott City's founding family. After World War I it served briefly as a veterans hospital, then resumed its civilian life until Lily Tyson Elliott died in 1924. Abandoned, it stood vacant until 1938, when a group of enthusiasts partially restored the mansion as a summer playhouse. In 1942 it was bought for another hotel project, which never materialized. In 1954 a former Secret Service agent rented the building and set up the Highland Manor nursing home. Four years later it was partially demolished and abandoned for a second time.

Over three decades the structure was invaded by weeds, fouled by graffiti, and haunted by thugs and, some said, by ghosts. Efforts to rescue the place began in the mid-'60s when a private group, the Friends of Patapsco Female Institute (FPFI), persuaded Howard County to buy the site. Initially the group dreamed of restoring the old manse to its original glory. Ideas were floated to use it as a cultural center, an arboretum, or a new home for county District Court. But the building's ongoing decay would have required radical surgery, hence today's deconstructed/reconstructed look.

In its present incarnation the old school is put to a growing variety of uses. FPFI, which still maintains the site, offers tours; archeology classes are taught at a dig on the grounds; weddings and other social events have been held. (Blessedly, the place is not cluttered with explanatory plaques and labels. That's what tours are for.) The ruins recently hosted a film series, which included, of all things, a screening of the classic 1943 version of *Jane Eyre*, starring Joan Fontaine and Orson Welles. Unfortunately regular visiting hours are limited: Sundays only, 1-4 p.m., April through October. (The institute's visitors center is open Tuesdays and Thursdays, 10 a.m. to 3 p.m.)

Surprisingly, the setting has not yet been used for live theater. With its wide stairs, Grecian columns, and gaping windows, the place might have been restored with *Oedipus Rex* or *Hamlet* in mind. Deborah Ing, FPFI's executive director, says the group has just received a state grant to help produce its first drama, a historical piece set in the institute's antebellum years. Dramaturges take note!

Tom Chalkley
August 5, 1998

Postscript: A play is now performed periodically at the Patapsco Female Institute ruins—Dear Old Patapsco, based on the diaries of institute students—but no other dramatic productions have been staged.

Bunny Trail

Before honoring a Bird, it housed the Bunnies. Such is the saga of 28 South Light Street.

Since 1993 the slender building at this address has been adorned with the looming likeness of Oriole Cal Ripken Jr. A sign company occupies the storefront beneath Cal's feet. Before that, local clothier Jos. A. Bank sold suits there. And before that—for a dozen mad, glad years—this unassuming building was the Baltimore Playboy Club, local outpost of centerfold king Hugh Hefner's silly, salacious empire.

Adjust, if you will, your mind-set to a time before brassieres were torched and the word "sexual" was teamed with "harassment." In a stretch of years bookended by Eisenhower's second term and the Summer of Love, Playboy, Inc. was a cultural force. The original Playboy Club opened in Chicago in 1960, just seven years after "Hef"—failed cartoonist and erstwhile circulation director for *Children's Activities* magazine—launched *Playboy* magazine with borrowed cash and three nude photos of Marilyn Monroe. The members-only club (you paid $50 to become a "key holder") offered cocktails, eats, and entertainment. But the real draw was the Bunnies—women in satin corsets with bunny ears on their heads and bunny tails on their heinies. Within a year the Chicago Playboy Club had locked in more than 106,000 members.

From this initial hutch other Playboy clubs bred like, well, rabbits—opening in New York, Miami, Los Angeles, and points in-between. Baltimore got its Bunnies in 1964 (though not without public protest from some irate local ladies). Bunnies reported to a Bunny Mother and boned up on Bunnyhood via a 44-page manual. ("Your proudest possession is your bunny tail," it informed. "You must make sure it is white and fluffy.") The manual was penned by the director of Bunny training—Hef's younger brother, Keith, whose previous claim to fame was starring in the Baltimore kiddie TV show *Mr. Toby and His Tip Top Merry Go Round.*

What kind of woman became a Bunny? All kinds, really. Debbie Harry and Lauren Hutton were Bunnies, as was arch-feminist Gloria Steinem (albeit to expose the horrors of the ear-and-tail trade). "It was the hardest job I ever had in my life—but also fun," says Ruth, a Baltimore Bunny from 1970 to '72 who asked that her last name be withheld. "You had to work in spike heels and an outfit wired like an old corset. If your breasts weren't big enough, you put a pair of pantyhose under them."

The club (remodeled in '69 after a six-alarm blaze) featured a Playmate Lounge on the first floor (where "Missy the Pool Bunny" shot billiards) and a penthouse nightclub where Billy Eckstine, Ethel Ennis, Flip Wilson, and Gabe Kaplan appeared. Sports figures Joe Namath, Bubba Smith, and Vida Blue were among the visitors.

"It's safe to say the club was glitzy," says Alan Shecter, who did public-relations work for Playboy from 1968 to '74. (Today he co-owns the Charles Theatre and nearby properties.) "When you walked inside, it woke you up."

Bonnie (who also asked that her last name not be used) began a six-month Baltimore Bunny stint in '65, when she was 17. She remembers serving drinks via the famous Bunny Dip (the tight, tiny costumes necessitated bending at the knees, not the waist). "We really got stuffed into those outfits," she says. "You couldn't sit down, you had to perch because of your tail. I didn't feel silly at the time, but there's no way I'd do it over again."

Of course, there's no way she could do it again. In the '70s the Playboy Club's trite titillation fell victim to a morphing sexual Zeitgeist: Women's lib was emerging on one end of the spectrum, hard-core porn on the other. The Playboy Clubs went from cash cows to dead meat. Baltimore's Bunny club went belly up in 1977. (The last U.S. Playboy Club, in Lansing,

Michigan, closed in 1988; a Filipino club survived until 1991.)

"Its heyday was already over when I started," Ruth says. "Dressing up like a rabbit to be a waitress? It was really styled for the '50s."

Was the Baltimore Playboy Club a dark page in pre-feminist history, or a largely innocent bit of red-meat-and-martini Americana?

"It's just politically not acceptable today," Shecter concedes. "There's a feeling that the women were exploited. But, if anything, they were doing the exploiting, since they were making men pay a living for themselves." But then, he never had to keep a tail white and fluffy.

Brennen Jensen
August 19, 1998

Upward Mobility

The stately rowhouse at 14 West Mount Vernon Place has its proper share of historic connections and architectural charms. It was built in 1890 by George Small, scion of one of Baltimore's great 19th-century mercantile and railroad dynasties. In 1897 it became the home of Theodore Marburg, tobacco heir, author, art connoisseur, pacifist, and diplomat, who served as U.S. ambassador to Belgium from 1912 to 1914. Marburg was a Washington insider and a great entertainer; at least two presidents, Woodrow Wilson and William Howard Taft, supped at the Mount Vernon mansion. Wilson is said to have drafted the original covenants of the League of Nations—the doomed precursor to the United Nations—on the premises. Taft was a longtime friend and a frequent visitor.

The building itself, still called the Marburg House, has all

the pomp of an embassy. On its pink granite stoop stand two ornate 7-foot cast-iron lamp stands adorned with lion's heads. The building's arched doorway and window frames are riddled with carvings, including two more lions' heads and the huge face of a satyr, whose leering expression seems somewhat out of keeping with the rest of the structure. Inside, a large wood-paneled lobby leads to a grand wooden staircase with a handrail as wide and smooth as a toddler's slide. Upstairs, the ceilings are decorated with floral plaster moldings, chandeliers the size of Christmas trees, and turn-of-the-century murals.

This house that railroading built is now the headquarters of Agora, Inc., a publishing company that owns a number of Baltimore properties. Dawne Coots, an accounting manager with the firm, serves as the building's de facto tour guide because her office space is in the lobby, tucked under the grand staircase. Coots' desk is half-hidden by a statue of the Roman god Mercury, sensuously clad in winged helmet, winged sandals, a small grape leaf, and nothing else.

"The building is so beautiful that people have a habit of coming in and asking for information," Coots says. "I work closest to the front door, so I had to learn the information just to entertain them." She cheerfully points out examples of Tiffany glass, identifies the honey-brown wood paneling as "South African bleached mahogany," and explains that, according to house lore, the singular, stout armchair in the lobby was custom-built to accommodate the famous girth of President Taft. Throughout the mansion, the number of hand-worked surfaces and hand-wrought objects is awe-inspiring, a testament to the huge fortunes of the owners (and to the relatively low pay of skilled artisans of a century ago).

In sum, the structure is one of the brighter, if lesser-known, gems in Mount Vernon's crown. But what sets the place apart from its neighbors is its smallest and least decorative space: the elevator. It's believed to be the oldest working elevator in Baltimore, and the city's first elevator in a private residence. Judging from its architectural enclosure, the elevator was part of the original structure, meaning that it has been going up and down for more than 100 years.

It is also, in all probability, the smallest passenger elevator in town, with a floor space of roughly 4 feet by 4 feet. Officially, the machine is rated for a capacity of three persons and a load limit of 600 pounds, but it's hard to imagine three adults squeezing into the Porta-John sized space unless they are intimate friends. "You go in with anything more than 600 pounds," Coots says, "and it starts sinking slowly to the bottom."

Unlike most of the building's features, the elevator is largely machine-made and utilitarian, with old but not antique fixtures and up-to-date permits. Normally it is hidden behind doors that have stained-glass windows. On the third floor, however, the stained glass is missing, replaced by clear glass that allows the visitor to watch the dusty cables, pulleys, and weights in action.

The elevator's modesty is oddly reassuring in a house that is otherwise encrusted with luxuries. Perhaps it's a reminder that even the most august persons take up only so much space—with the exception of President Taft, who probably took the stairs.

Tom Chalkley
October 14, 1998

The Birds

Each year, with the onset of winter, Baltimore City Hall and the neighboring courthouse buildings become roosting sites for thousands of starlings. By day, the stubby, omnivorous birds fan out across downtown in small groups, pecking at any digestible substance they can find. But as evening nears, they rush toward the old buildings and stake out perches for the night among the ledges, sills, and cornices. Their collective cacophony of whistles, chirps, and peeps can be heard over the rush-hour traffic.

In December and January, the influx of starlings roughly coincides with the 4:30 p.m. exodus of city employees. "They come out at dusk, so when you leave the building you hear this noise. At first you don't realize what it is, and then you look up," City Hall curator Jeanne March Davis says. The building's white facade is peppered with the squat, squealing critters, and the sky surrounding its mansard roof is aswirl with them; Davis says it reminds her of the winged monkeys from *The Wizard of Oz.*

Davis has worked in the building for 17 years, organizing art exhibits and seeing to the décor. The starlings have been there every winter of her tenure. Although the birds' acidic droppings are corrosive to the building's marble surfaces, Davis finds the annual winter visitation "really kinda neat…. It's part of the experience of working at City Hall."

According to Baltimore naturalist Anneke Davis (no relation to Jeanne March Davis), the starlings' habit of roosting in vast numbers on winter evenings is probably a defensive measure against predators and the cold. (During the spring and summer months, when starlings are nesting and raising their young, they congregate in much smaller groups.) Beginning in late September, they form flocks that can literally darken portions of the sky. In rural and suburban areas, they stream into dense forests and thickets for their nightly roosts, but huge urban infestations of the birds are common throughout North America and the starlings' native Europe. City centers, Anneke Davis explains, make attractive roosting zones because they are warmer than areas with less pavement and traffic; City Hall and the courthouses, with their ornate pre-modern architecture, offer the sort of high-density perching surfaces starlings prefer.

Whatever the location, once starlings settle on their winter lodgings they are difficult to budge. Small towns besieged by the birds have used buckshot, fireworks, recordings of bird distress calls, and "propane exploders" (which make loud noises to scare away the birds) with limited success. In downtown Baltimore, maintenance crews have had to find alternatives to noise-making strategies; they've tried "bird remover"—a sticky substance starlings find offensive—and nonlethal 110-volt wires called "bird chasers," to no avail. Like the famed swallows of Capistrano, Baltimore's feathered rats come back every year. In this respect, downtown Baltimore has it worse than rural areas, where starlings tend to shift around from year to year.

These days, there are actually consultants who can advise architects on how to prevent noxious bird invasions, but when City Hall was built in 1875, the starling problem was not anticipated. *Sturnus vulgaris* didn't even arrive in this country until 1890, when—legend has it—a man named Eugene Scheifflin took on the bizarre project of importing to America a sampling of every bird species mentioned in the works of Shakespeare. Scheifflin released 80 starlings in New York's Central Park, and the fertile, adaptable creatures have been expanding their range ever since. By 1900, when Baltimore's courthouse was dedicated, there were starlings in New Jersey and Connecticut. The aggressive birds now blanket the continent, the bane of woodpeckers and bluebirds, whose nests the starlings target for takeover.

It's tempting to see their huge, unaccountable gatherings as omens, or—especially at City Hall—as mocking allegories of the chattering humans inside the walls. Listen closely to starlings, and their rapid vocalizations sound disturbingly like human speech. In fact, according to the *Audubon Encyclopedia of North American Birds*, starlings "freely imitate other birds and environmental noises and, as a result, have a very varied vocabulary, much of which consists of harsh and discordant notes." This dubious talent was noted by Shakespeare, who wrote in part one of *Henry IV*, "I'll have a starling shall be taught to speak." It's the Bard's sole mention of the bird.

Tom Chalkley
January 6, 1999

Trains of Thought

I would venture that any nature lover can trace his or her roots back to one special place where they first encountered the power of wilderness. For me, that spot is Robert E. Lee Park, more commonly known as Lake Roland.

Sure, I've seen more impressive places (the Adirondacks, the Alps, the Pacific Northwest), but—and it's a little embarrassing to admit this—for me, nothing compares to the six miles of shoreline along this man-made lake that sediment runoff is turning into a swamp. It was here, off Falls Road just north of the city line, that I developed the feeling that nature can provide a sense of adventure and historic discovery.

I first laid eyes on the place in my middle-school years, during a late-summer bike ride. I was bored out of my mind, ready to write the whole summer break off as a loss, when I came upon the park. I figured it must have been named after Robert E. Lee for a reason. My imagination supplied one when I discovered the abandoned railroad tracks running through the park. I pictured Civil War skirmishes and Rebel raiding parties, and hidden artifacts just waiting to be found. I followed the rails through the brush as if I'd stumbled on the ruins of a lost society. I was terribly disappointed when I found my way to Falls Road and the onrushing traffic.

I'd later discover that the tracks were merely remnants of the Northern Central Railway, and the park's name was the result of a philanthropist's request rather than the marking of a historical event. Nonetheless, from that day forward I developed a love for historical wreckage. Give me the ruins of an old grist mill drowning in vines and my imagination starts churning. I prefer my history raw, with no metal markers.

Sure, my logical, civic-minded half believes in historic preservation, but my artistic side greedily digs the patina of ruin. Walking those old railroad tracks is like coming upon a forgotten Jones Falls Expressway that's turned into one long trellis for weeds. I think about the passenger cars hurtling through this tunnel of tree limbs toward Baltimore and get as close as I ever will to time travel. But after a recent stroll, I figured it was time to spoil the illusion and dig through the written record of newspaper clippings and old documents, to get some real history to go with the imagined one.

As it turns out, there was some relatively minor Civil War action here, or at least hereabouts: In 1861, Baltimore Mayor George William Brown—vexed by the federal occupation of his city—directed police and Rebel sympathizers to tear up some of Northern Central's tracks (though not the ones in the park), according to *The Story of the Northern Central Railway* by Robert L. Gunnarsson, which was published in 1991.

More discoveries: There was a train station called Relay (not to be confused with the existing community of Relay, near Catonsville) at the southern tip of the lake, just west of where the light rail runs now; it burned down in the 1930s. On July 4, 1854, a brutal train wreck occurred three-quarters of a mile north of the Relay station; two trains full of day-trippers collided. The crash killed 35 people and injured more than 100.

Perhaps it's fitting that, while the mighty Baltimore and Ohio Railroad has its own museum, little remains of the Northern Central, a much-loved underdog in its day, according to Gunnarsson.

The Northern Central started out as the Baltimore and Susquehanna in 1828, a year after the founding of the B&O. While the B&O went west, the B&S headed north along Jones Falls. The stretch of tracks through what is now Robert E. Lee Park was known as the Green Spring Valley line. In 1832, according to Gunnarsson, horse-drawn carriages trotted up the rails to Relay, where a fresh team was hitched and headed toward the Green Spring Hotel and station. But the Green Spring line was destined to be a secondary line—the B&S opened another northbound route from Cockeysville through Monkton and into York, Pennsylvania. This became the main rail route out of Baltimore for the Northern Central, which arose out of a merger between the B&S and another railroad company. The Northern Central was taken over by the Pennsylvania Rail Road, which ran up into the coal-rich areas of northern Pennsylvania; occasionally, walking along Lake Roland, you can still find bits of coal and smelted iron ore.

At its peak, though, the Northern Central was a commuter system, linking rural Maryland communities to Baltimore. Twenty-seven trains each day ran between downtown and

Mount Washington, and lines such as the Parkton Local and the Ruxton Rocket developed loyal followings. As the 20th century advanced and cars became more ubiquitous, the Northern Central Commuters Association and the state Public Service Commission wrangled with the company to keep the passenger lines open.

But they were only delaying the inevitable; ridership continued to dwindle through the 1950s. The Northern Central's final commuter run came on June 27, 1959. Long-distance passenger trains continued to use the tracks until 1972, when Hurricane Agnes wrecked the rails.

Now, this pioneering vein of early American commercial railroading is the domain of mountain bikers and dog walkers; only the occasional unidentified piece of foundation or length of wooden bridge reveal clues to the park's history. But there's still the sense of discovery here, the feeling that you might stumble on some relic or long-forgotten story. That sense of discovery will always bring me back.

Charles Cohen
April 7, 1999

Armory Show

Yes, those are gun ports spaced along the Fifth Regiment Armory's undulating gray walls. Those little notches serve only as aesthetic touches today, but when the granite edifice looming just south of Bolton Hill was built nearly 100 years ago, they were designed—had the situation warranted—to bristle with gun barrels. The armory was a well-armed, well-manned fortress in the heart of Baltimore.

Don't look for guns today as you tool down Howard Street

along the stone building's east facade. Though it remains the headquarters of the Maryland National Guard, there are hardly any weapons, munitions, or soldiers left in the armory, according to Capt. Drew Sullins. It's mostly offices now—military folk wielding computer keyboards, not carbines.

Sunbeams stream down through arched windows within the vast main hall, landing on a wooden floor that's larger than a football field. All is calm within the cavernous space. But back in 1912, more than 20,000 folks packed in here for a riotous Democratic Party convention, where Woodrow Wilson fought for—and eventually won—the nomination for president. And they had a hot time here back in 1933, when the building was engulfed in an 11-alarm fire that obliterated everything but the stout granite walls. Nineteen years later, the reconstructed building was the site of more pandemonium when a hastily erected grandstand collapsed during a Sonja Henie ice show, injuring more than 270 spectators. (Henie later faced a costly legal settlement.) Quiet now, the old armory has a formidable history—along with a few secrets.

"I've heard stories that years ago, when the train station was where the [Maryland Institute] art school is now, they had tunnels from here to the station," Sullins says. "They could get troops to the trains in secrecy if they had to mobilize and get out of town."

When its last stone was laid in 1903, the castlelike structure was the nation's largest armory. It rose on a midtown bluff that was formerly the site of a handsome manor home called Bolton (from which the stately adjacent neighborhood draws its name). Long before the construction of Baltimore's arena or convention center, the armory hall hosted a variety of events: circuses, dog shows, dances, wrestling matches, and the like. The walls echoed with the music of Louis Armstrong, Duke Ellington, and Ella Fitzgerald. As recently as 1994, troops were billeted here, and they still drill here occasionally. During wartime many a Baltimorean walked through the armory's bronzed entrance and marched out as a freshly inducted soldier.

My brief tour ends where the reek of history is the strongest: the Maryland National Guard Museum, a series of rooms brimming with artifacts highlighting more than 200 years of Maryland military history. (Sullins and the museum's curator, Sgt. Scott Gostomski, must flip on the lights for my visit; the museum is open by appointment only.)

One room covers the weapons and wardrobe of the Civil War, while another shows more contemporary items from the Persian Gulf War. The largest space is dedicated to World War II, displaying captured weapons. (There's a German "burp" gun, named for the sound it makes, and even a Hitler Youth dagger for the littlest Nazis.) Most of the pieces have been donated by local veterans, particularly members of the 29th Infantry Division—heavily stocked with Marylanders—which stormed Omaha Beach during the Normandy invasion.

"It's a shame we don't have the money to open the museum all the time," Sullins says. "This is a little secret in Baltimore nobody knows about. When *Saving Private Ryan* came out, I guarantee this place could have been packed with people because these are the units that landed on D-Day."

There's even a jeep on display that landed on the beaches. It was used by Maj. Gen. Gerhardt, but bigger brass also rode shotgun in the humble craft. Sullins points to a photo showing Eisenhower himself reviewing troops from the olive-drab vehicle. (Five years ago the jeep was flown back to Normandy to take part in the festivities surrounding the 50th anniversary of the landings.)

Taking a break from his tour-guide duties, Sullins scrambles into the historic vehicle's passenger seat. He looks pretty good up there, clad as he is in camouflage fatigues. Of course, the two bars on his shoulder mark him several ranks short of the jeep's more storied passengers. But then that's probably why the captain is grinning.

"I like sitting here where Eisenhower sat," Sullins says. "It's pretty cool."

(For an appointment to see the Maryland National Guard Museum, call [410] 576-1441.)

Brennen Jensen
May 5, 1999

Royal Treatment

We're in Upton, on the corner of Pennsylvania and Lafayette avenues. There's a small plaza of cracked cement surrounding a fountain containing glass shards and a bag-wrapped bottle—but no water. Beyond the cement stretches a baseball field where the spring heat wave has blanched the grass the color of dirty straw.

"This is sacred ground," says George Gilliam, chairman of the Pennsylvania Avenue Committee, who is serving as my tour guide.

Gilliam is 46, just old enough to remember a different vista along this stretch. He recalls when the block was dominated by a looming brick theater with arched windows and a glowing marquee reading ROYAL. It was a fitting name for the 1,300-seat theater that for more than three decades hosted the royalty of the African-American entertainment world: Duke Ellington, Count Basie, Ella Fitzgerald, the Supremes, the Temptations, and countless others.

"I saw James Brown there, must have been 1965," Gilliam says. "I was young, but I remember people were lined up all the way around the corner."

The Royal fell to the wrecking ball in 1971. In its glory years, though, it was Baltimore's version of Harlem's storied (and still standing) Apollo Theater. And up until the '60s,

Pennsylvania Avenue was Baltimore's Lennox Avenue: the commercial and entertainment epicenter for the city's African-American community. Then came decades of social change and urban renewal.

Where's the Penn Hotel, the city's first black-owned inn, where many of the Royal's performers stayed when Jim Crow laws barred them from lodging downtown?

"It used to be up there on the corner," Gilliam says, waving his arm northward. "It was torn down."

What became of the Regent, Pennsylvania Avenue's other grand theater, once the second largest in the city?

"They tore that down, too."

And the Albert Auditorium? The Strand Ballroom? Ike Dixon's Comedy Club, where a starry-eyed kid named Sammy Davis once sang for free?

"All torn down."

Across from the defunct fountain sits an homage to the area's better days: a bronze statue of Billie Holiday, posed in midsong. You can almost hear her visceral, blues-drenched voice bemoaning the state of the sacred ground.

"I heard people were taking tour groups up here and pointing to that empty field and saying, 'That's where the great Royal Theater was,'" Gilliam says. "I found that absolutely shameful."

But Gilliam didn't just get mad—he got busy. Three years ago the mayor's office tapped him to help it develop activities for the African-American community in conjunction with the city's 1997 bicentennial celebration. Gilliam did some research and discovered, as he puts it, that "everything led to Pennsylvania Avenue." In June of '97 he resurrected a long-dead spectacle: the annual Cadillac Parade. From the 1950s to the early '70s, dressing to the nines and parading down the street in a fine Caddy was an annual Pennsylvania Avenue event. (Elaborate Easter and Halloween parades were also part of the street's golden years.) Upwards of 37,000 people came for the parade that summer and the musical block party that followed it.

"The response was tremendous," Gilliam says. "It showed that folks would come back to this neighborhood."

The parade and party are now annual events, collectively known as the Historic Cadillac Parade and the Royal Theater Show. On June 19, Caddies and vintage cars of other makes (no Lexuses or Infinitis, please) will again tool down Pennsylvania Avenue, ending up at the "sacred ground" where the Royal once stood, and where numerous musical acts, including bluesman Big Jesse Yawn and the Dunbar Jazz Band, will perform.

As successful as the parade and party became, Gilliam and the committee he helped form still went looking for a permanent way to preserve and promote the area's rich history. Enter the Royal Theater Project, which will replace the broken fountain with a two-story replica of the Royal's marquee. The names of the dozens of famed performers who played the theater will scroll across the marquee electronically. The state has already ponied up $100,000 for the cause, and Gilliam hopes to break ground late this summer. He believes the marquee will become a tour-bus destination—and, potentially, a gateway to an area on the rebound.

"I want people to get a taste of the African-American experience here, just as you can get a taste of the Italian-American experience in Little Italy," Gilliam says. "We're reaching backwards for the future."

Brennen Jensen
June 16, 1999

Postscript: Ground was broken on the replica Royal marquee at the June 2000 Cadillac parade, and the project is expected to be completed in 2001.

Hog Heaven

Daniels' Bar is classic reporter bait. The bungalow structure, with its open-air bar graced by a row of motorcycles, sits on a rather dangerous-looking curve of Route 1 in Elkridge. The riders stand around grinning into their beers in a cloud of diesel smoke and road grit. And they're enjoying a truly rare drink: According to owner Dan Daniels, the tavern is the last open-air roadside bar in Maryland. It's an irresistible image for any wandering scribe—a perfect photo op, a piece of roadside Americana. *National Geographic*, *The Christian Science Monitor*, *The Sun*, even the crew of TV's *Homicide* have all stopped in for the flavor.

I've wanted to do this story since 1982. That's when I use to take the Greyhound home from the University of Maryland at College Park; Route 1's weed-choked drive-ins, cheap motels, and storefront fortune-tellers provided a picture show across my window along the way. But nothing caught my attention like the roadside biker bar.

Seventeen years later, I've reached my destination. The outdoor bar is empty when I arrive one late afternoon, but a few patrons are in the tavern behind it, along with the owner.

Daniels stands 6-foot-5; he looks like the Marlboro Man and talks like him, too. He and I share a dish of stale candies as he does his best to piece together the ragtag history of the place.

Daniels and his mother, Emily Daniels, bought the bar 25 years ago from a couple named John and Geraldine Pearl; before that, it was owned by a family named Kugel (or some such; Daniels doesn't know the spelling). Emily still cooks up the meals in the tavern's kitchen; Daniels' son, Dan Jr., works behind the bar.

No one seems to know exactly when the place opened for

business, but as the story goes, drink was being dispensed at the location long before there was a bar. Dan Daniels says a past owner of the place, his name long forgotten, kept a still out back, and "all his friends sat down on his front porch and drank his hooch." The man eventually got a liquor license and set up the outdoor bar, Daniels says.

The current owner doesn't know when local motorcyclists started making the bar/restaurant their pit stop, but he is certain of one thing: Daniels' isn't a "biker bar."

"We don't like the term 'biker,'" he says. "It refers to a negative image." And an incorrect one, he asserts: "Been here 25 years, never had to call the police."

Daniels calls out to the few patrons sitting at tables. All of them are riders. He asks what they do for a living. Computer salesman, business owner, unemployed. The one thing all motorcyclists do seem to have in common is image-consciousness. In each of several trips to the bungalow bar, the first thing I hear is that motorcyclists have gotten a bad rap.

"It looks scary," Nick Hernick, who chugged up on a Harley-Davidson, says of the bar, "but it's not at all."

To a nonrider, Daniels' Bar can seem a bit intimidating, with its phalanx of bikes parked in a precise line, wheels swung to the south, and the proliferation of leather and tattoos among the patrons. But the sight of a Nissan Sentra pulling into the parking lot draws only a few stares, no glares. And the row of motorcycles is a mix of Hondas and Harleys, their respective riders—deadly enemies, if one believes the biker hype—sharing a beer in harmony. In fact, some riders own both foreign and domestic bikes. Glenn Vidal, a vice president of a security company, comes cruising in on a Honda Shadow; his Harley's at home.

"When I get home my suit comes off, my doo rag comes on, and I turn into my little biker self," says Vidal, who has been riding since he bought a Vespa scooter at the age of 14.

Parked nearby is Mike Weiner's '87 Harley Softail, custom

built to ride low, with a sissy bar, a bullet hole painted on the tank, and a helmet bearing the slogan HELMET LAWS SUCK.

Weiner's a purist. He used to sell Harleys, but he got sick of seeing "RUBs"—rich urban bikers—writing out $15,000 checks for new bikes he was used to selling to people who'd saved for years for the treasured purchase. Now he makes his living driving a truck. But when he's not working, he's on two wheels. "You can go anywhere on your bike and people will come over and talk to you," he says. "You can be the biggest dirtbag in the world and they'll come up to you and ask you about your bike."

Weiner, like so many Harley riders, remains loyal to hogs, but not much brand-name bashing goes on at Daniels'—at least not out loud. Maybe that's why the place attracts bikers like a gas station on a lonely interstate draws long-distance travelers—from a man claiming to be Hulk Hogan's brother to motorcycle-loving U.S. Sen. Ben Nighthorse Campbell of Colorado.

Dan Daniels has become a sort of unofficial advocate and den father for local riders. He's still pushing for the elimination of Maryland's helmet law. He organizes scavenger hunts known as "poker runs," in which riders cruise back roads looking for appointed stops; there, they have to find Daniels' selected souvenirs and carry them back to the bar.

It was at Daniels', the owner says, that the idea of the Toy Run was hatched. For 17 years, motorcyclists rallied by the thousands at the bar with Christmas gifts for underprivileged children and joined a thunderous procession riding into Baltimore. Hanging over a doorway of the restaurant is a panoramic photo of the 1987 rally that attracted an estimated 40,000 riders.

But those days are over. This past year, hassles such as the high cost of police escorts for the run forced the organizers to shut it down, Daniels says. But he remains the keeper of another endangered tradition: the open-air bar where you can ride up, get a drink, and sit by your bike. It's where his patrons seem most comfortable, and most natural.

Charles Cohen
June 23, 1999

Mysterious Island

Key Bridge commuters, boaters, and anglers see it every day, but if you're not used to it, Fort Carroll is weird. Crouched in the bridge's shadow, the six-sided island fortress seems eerily medieval; even on bright days, its sooty stone walls and dense overgrowth are dark. Posted along its dilapidated landing pier, NO TRESPASSING signs warn off would-be visitors.

Submerged debris makes the approach to the fort difficult to navigate. Onshore—if one can say a man-made island has a shore—gaping holes in the pavement can snare the unwary trespasser. The entire 3.45-acre ruin is completely deserted. Its vacant gun ports stare out over the Patapsco River like eye sockets in a skull. Cue the *Twilight Zone* theme.

Fort Carroll's gloomy looks reflect its many disappointments rather than its auspicious beginnings in the mid-19th century. Named for Charles Carroll, Maryland's famed signer of the Declaration of Independence, the midriver fort seemed a logical way to prevent a replay of 1814, when the British navy besieged Fort McHenry. To design and supervise the project, the Army Corps of Engineers tapped Robert E. Lee, then a brevet colonel who had recently distinguished himself in the Mexican War. For the proposed fort, Lee set about creating an island just north of the harbor's main channel, off Soller's Point.

The plan was to build a hexagonal sea wall rising 40 feet off the river bottom, enclosing a sort of four-tiered pyramid of platforms for 350 cannons. In 1848, the year after Lee's hire, pilings were driven into the muddy shallows. On top of the pilings engineers laid a 4-acre foundation that, with the help of a diving bell, they weighed down with thousands of tons of stone. For three years, during construction of the fort, Lee lived at 908 West Madison Avenue. (He is said to have been a gracious neighbor who romped with local children and wore his full dress uniform to social functions.)

In 1851, after putting $1 million into the project, Congress cut off funds for Fort Carroll before it was completed. New technology had rendered the project obsolete. Powerful, accurate new guns had been invented, guns capable of reducing the fort to rubble in a few hours. When the money ran dry, only the fort's sea wall and the battery's first tier were complete.

The very next year Lee was called away to serve as superintendent of the U.S. Military Academy at West Point. And then somebody noticed that Fort Carroll was sinking. (It would go on sinking for 40 years.) The engineering tour de force had become a white elephant.

Military authorities found a few uses for Fort Carroll: a base for a lighthouse (needed to warn ships away from the fort itself), a site for target practice, a source of scrap iron. Of the 350 cannons planned for the fort, only six were ever placed. One cannon remains on the island today, cemented in an upright position to serve as a mooring post.

As the years dragged on, Baltimoreans proposed an array of civilian reuses for the island, including two separate statues, a marina, a duty-free port of entry, and a prison, among other things. William F. Broening, mayor from 1919 to 1923, proposed erecting a giant electric WELCOME TO BALTIMORE sign there, but sadly, it never came to pass.

The last great hopes for Fort Carroll arose in 1958 when Benjamin Eisenberg, a Baltimore lawyer, purchased the island from the Army Corps of Engineers for $10,010. Eisenberg and his sons repaired and painted masonry, planted fruit trees, exterminated rats, and generally made the place hospitable. They hoped to develop a restaurant on the island, but the plan fell through. Undaunted, the Eisenbergs proposed that Fort Carroll be used to support a bridge across the Patapsco—and a bridge-accessible motel. But when Key Bridge was built in the mid-'70s, its right-of-way lay a half-mile west of the island. (Eisenberg's heirs, who still own the island, declined to be interviewed for this story.)

Today the unused, unfinished fort reminds us of history's vagaries. Like Lee's Rebel offensive in the 1860s, it was a massive, costly, archaic scheme, outflanked by military-industrial progress. Think of it as a monument that, rather than commemorating the Civil War, foreshadowed it. Who knows? Like the South, Fort Carroll may rise again.

Tom Chalkley
July 21, 1999

Lounge Acts

*A*h, the Club Charles, "America's ace of clubs," where sharp-dressed Baltimoreans dined and danced in an atmosphere of urbane sophistication. A posh place where well-heeled couples would down crab imperial and a few deftly mixed Manhattans, then sit back and enjoy Tony Bennett crooning "Because of You" from a spot-lit stage.

No, I'm not talking about today's Club Charles—the smoky, jukebox-booming hipster bar across the street from the Charles Theatre. The original Club Charles was four blocks south, at the northwest corner of Charles and Preston streets. Debuting in 1941, it was a foremost gem in Baltimore's rollicking, decade-long nightclub era.

What to do on a Saturday night? Back then it was simple: Dress up and step out. What passes for our so-called lounge revival is mostly a generation of campy retro-heads pining wistfully for the days of swank supper clubs, bracing cocktails, cigarette girls, and floor shows. Seventy-six-year-old Gilbert Sandler, erstwhile *Evening Sun* local-history columnist (and still an occasional *Sun* contributor), doesn't have to imagine such an era. He had a date with his future wife at the Club Charles in the late '40s.

"It felt big-time to be there," Sandler recalls. "There was a large, well-dressed crowd. You had the feeling Baltimore was going big time. We had our own New York-style supper club."

The Club Charles also figured in the love life of controversial comic Lenny Bruce, whose biting social commentary and obscene (by 1950s standards) language revolutionized American popular culture. Bruce was on his way up when he played the club in 1951, having won a televised Arthur Godfrey talent contest just three years earlier. (Conversely, the Club Charles was on its way down—it closed in '52.) After his final set, Bruce wandered over to a nearby coffee shop and met his future wife—busty, red-headed Hot Honey Harlowe, who had been parading her ample curves at a local burlesque bar. (The story goes that they stayed up all night prank-calling hapless Baltimoreans picked at random from the phone book.)

The Club Charles occupied the corner of a staid, buff-colored four-story building. Erected in 1927 as the headquarters of the Knights of Pythias fraternal group, it later housed a Studebaker showroom. Today, the edifice is home to a Crestar bank; nary a trace remains of the luxurious nightspot that hosted everyone from Carmen Miranda and Milton Berle to the Tic-Toc dancers and Yvette Dare and her performing parrot.

If the Club Charles had a rival in this glamorous age, it was the Chanticleer, four blocks south at the corner of Charles and

Eager. While the Club Charles is gone without a trace, the Chanticleer (a medieval term for rooster) is still very much with us. Since 1972 it's housed the Hippo, one of the city's largest and most popular gay and lesbian bars. Built as a cocktail lounge in 1939, the building's curved cement exterior is one of the city's best (and few remaining) examples of art-deco architecture. The interior was a study in dramatic, recessed fluorescent lighting. A *Baltimore News-Post* columnist called the lounge an "answer to an architect's dreams" and praised the deep-pile carpets, white leather lounge chairs, shell-pink ceiling, and walls of contrasting shades of blue: "It's an outstanding pleasure spot...dedicated to the enjoyment of life through better drinking."

At the center of the sunken, oval bar was a revolving glass podium where the entertainers performed while dramatically lit from below. This glowing spot saw the likes of Merv Griffin, Sid Caesar, Zero Mostel, Walter Winchell, and Henny Youngman. The "swingsational" Four-Toppers served as house band. In 1945, the club advertised the appearance of "the fellow who's setting the country on fire with his out-of-the-world ballad song-singing." The fellow was Dean Martin. Ironically, the night before Dino opened, the Chanticleer hosted a lanky 19-year-old funnyman named Jerry Lewis. (Call it a Hollywood near-miss; a few months later Martin and Lewis paired up and became the country's most popular comedy team.)

The Chanticleer's lights dimmed in the '50s. The deco lounge later became a restaurant (the One West) and a catering hall. By the time the Hippo debuted, little was left of the '30s-chic interior. (The main bar area is now a dance floor.) Even the decorative rooster has rusted off the weather vane that still tops the Charles Street entrance that's no longer in use.

So what to do on a Saturday night? Our glamorous options are few these days. Many forces caused the demise of the downtown supper clubs: the rise of television, the rise of suburbia, the rise in entertainers' pay. To this list Sandler adds one more item.

"We all started having these club basements," he says. "And we just stayed in them."

Brennen Jensen
August 25, 1999

Tales From the Crypt

I BRAKE FOR OLD GRAVEYARDS reads a bumper sticker on Wayne Schaumburg's Subaru. And indeed he does. Trooping through moldering cemeteries is Schaumburg's idea of fun.

But the bespectacled 53-year-old is not obsessed with death. It's an interest in history, not the hereafter, that brings him to the old boneyards. And it's a history lesson that has brought me and about 30 other folks through Green Mount Cemetery's Tudor Gothic gatehouse this crisp Saturday morning. Schaumburg is conducting a two-hour tour of this grand dame of city graveyards.

"This is ground zero for Baltimore history," he says of the 68-acre midtown cemetery, where he's led tours for 15 years. "All of the city's movers and shakers are here."

Glancing down at his dog-eared note cards, Schaumburg explains that when Green Mount opened in 1839 it was only the fourth "urban rural" cemetery in the nation, offering a parklike setting close to the countryside. "They were an alternative to the cramped, hemmed-in churchyard burial grounds," he says, in a resonant voice befitting someone who taught history in city schools for 32 years.

From Green Mount Cemetery's inception in 1839, anyone could be buried there. Nineteenth-century Baltimore might have been stratified along religious, ethnic, and racial lines in life, but

not in death (though the high costs—$100 a plot when Green Mount opened—proved an economic restriction). The sylvan resting place proved so popular that many families transferred their departed loved ones from the city's older graveyards.

"That sounds a little ghoulish in 1999," Schaumburg says. "But if you see a date of death here before 1839, you know that's what happened."

Our tour group is on the move, strolling down leaf-strewn paths along rows of marble angels, urns, columns, and obelisks. The Victorians were somewhat squeamish about death, Schaumburg notes; many monuments use euphemism like "fell asleep" or "went to his rest" instead of "died." Though some headstones are weather-beaten, the cemetery as a whole is in excellent shape. (Schaumburg credits Green Mount's lofty stone walls with keeping vandals at bay.)

We pause at Enoch Pratt's red granite obelisk, which stands out amid all the white marble. We stroll past tin-can mogul Thomas Kensett Jr.'s grave, and the resting places of two

Baltimore mayors, Thomas Swann (who also did time as governor of Maryland) and Ferdinand Latrobe. "He was elected mayor seven times," Schaumburg says of Latrobe, "a record even Willie Don [Schaefer] never beat."

The Walters plot is next—the graves of produce-seller-turned-liquor-distributor-turned-art-collector William Walters and his son Henry. After sketching out the Walters saga, Schaumberg announces, "We've been speaking a lot about men. Let's turn our attention to a famous woman." He leads us through dew-damp grass to Elizabeth Patterson's marble slab, which reads AFTER LIFE'S FITFUL FEVER, SHE SLEEPS WELL—fitting words for the women who married Jerome Bonaparte, only to end up living alone after his big brother Napoleon annulled the marriage.

We skirt a looming mausoleum erected in 1929 (Bromo-Seltzer inventor Isaac Emerson is one of the notables resting within) and stop at the Whitridge family plot, site of Green Mount's first burial. A modest headstone marks the passing of Olivia Cushing Whitridge, a 2-year-old who died December 7, 1839. South of here, a brownstone chapel was erected at the cemetery's loftiest point in 1858. Copied from a chapel in Edinburgh, Scotland, the spire-topped edifice is locked up these days, but its basement houses a functioning crematorium. (Green Mount performs approximately 1,000 cremations a year.) The ground around the chapel hosts another slew of notables.

"No, that's not the grave of a hockey player," Schaumburg says in introducing *Sun* founder Arunah S. Abell's tomb, whose ornately carved monument is protected with a Plexiglas shield. The carving was done by Hugh Sisson, one of the cemetery's most prolific marble men. (Sound familiar? The carver's namesake great-grandson is a local microbrewer and co-host of WJHU-FM's *Cellar Notes*.) Other celebs by the chapel include Johns Hopkins, railroad mogul John W. Garrett, and governors Theodore McKeldin (buried next to wife Honolulu) and Albert Ritchie.

The tour ends at Green Mount's most famous (and

infamous) marker, a towering obelisk bearing the name BOOTH. It honors Junius Brutus Booth, but son and assassin John Wilkes is buried here, too. Schaumburg says it's not uncommon to find pennies placed on the marker (Lincoln side up, of course). Once he discovered an ornate red-white-and-blue flower arrangement bearing the words A GREAT AMERICAN in the Booth plot.

So many dead people, so little time. In two hours we've met some big names but made only a small dent in Green Mount's sprawling acreage, eternal home for more than 66,000 people. Crowded though the cemetery is, a few scattered grave sights are available. By way of parting, Schaumburg says he wouldn't mind "sleeping" here one day himself.

"I already know what I want on my headstone," he adds with a grin. "My name and the words 'I'm history.'"

Brennen Jensen
October 13, 1999

Postscript: Wayne Schaumburg gives Green Mount Cemetery tours in the spring and fall. Call (410) 256-2180 for dates and times.

Polka Parlor

Oompah music drifts into the liquor store. A couple dances beside the dusty, half-empty shelves. They're alone, save for an old yellow dog named Lady, who barks strenuously at no one in particular.

On the other side of the saloon door in the back, though, there's a crowd.

That's where the polka music is coming from—the barroom in the back, the Canton Liquor House.

The bar is hidden, speakeasy style; a passerby strolling

along Fleet Street in Fells Point would never know that, at least once a week, this joint jumps, mostly with elderly Polish-Americans who turn Saturday afternoons at the Canton Liquor House into a party. Men and women sing lustily along with the band, belying the grim feel that too often permeates Baltimore's old-timer bars. An ex-cop whoops at the musicians. An ex-postal worker plays the drums. An ex-street cleaner (Italian, but welcome) saws on a fiddle.

The true maestro in this group stands behind the bar, serving up $1.25 beers. Walter Stankowski, better known as "Lucky," has soft eyes and the bartender's wisdom that comes with pouring drinks for more than half a century. Stankowski has spent 54 of his 75 years running the Canton Liquor House, which his father owned before him. He's watched as his proud Polish neighborhood was overrun by strangers.

When Stankowski was growing up, the area now called Fells Point was known as the Foot of Broadway, a place where he learned to swim along the piers "and catch crabs—and my god, the crabs were monsters." His father bought the bar in 1944; the now-defunct American Brewing Company paid for its fixtures, an arrangement that was common between breweries and bars in the years after Prohibition, to help re-establish watering holes. (The old fixtures are no longer used, but they're still there.) Mighty trains used to run right down Fleet Street, then called Canton Avenue (hence the bar's name). Stankowski recalls how his family and others from the neighborhood would go out into the country every summer and work picking vegetables to pay off their credit at Hecht's Reliable, a local department store on Broadway.

"See, I was just a kid," he says. "And being a kid, it was all an adventure, like a Huckleberry Finn kind of thing."

During the week, the bar is nearly empty and there's plenty of time to go over the old days. Come Saturday, it's a different story. Former neighbors who've long since moved away come back. Fans of Polish music from as far away as Annapolis are weekend regulars. Gino Wysocki, a neighborhood kid who grew up to be a neighborhood cop (now retired), routinely makes the trip in from Dundalk. The popularity of the weekend polka jams has kept the Canton Liquor House in business, and helped Stankowski get through the loss of his wife of 48 years, Katherine, who died last year, just before the couple was to move into what he calls "my dream house" in Highlandtown.

Stankowski credits Kolegi (Polish for "friends"), the loosely formed band that gigs here Saturdays, for injecting not only a new life but a new outlook into the bar. Kolegi's roots go back a couple of years, when Tony Netzel starting coming in with his accordion and his memory bank full of Polish songs. A few weeks later, in came Gilbert Nadolny with his banjo. The duo was joined by Joe Kalinowski, who drummed in a local rock 'n' roll band called the Velvetones in the '60s but hadn't played in eight years. Then came Ernie Moch and his concertina, and Joseph Detota, the Italian fiddle player.

Canton Liquor House is one of the last remnants of the old

neighborhood, observes Dot Siemek. Siemek once co-owned (with her husband, Bill) another local landmark—Siemek's Meat Market across the street, which is now closed but was in business for 50 years and was famous for the pig sign hanging over its door. Siemek seems ready to wallow morosely in nostalgia, but the careening beat demands happiness. Within a few songs she's standing over the bar shaking a rack of bells, claiming the exercise tones her torso.

These days, there's no telling what will happen at the once-moribund bar. One recent Saturday a guitarist and a sax player dropped in and joined Kolegi for a few numbers. The band joyrode from rhumbas to waltzes, a little jazz here and a little country there. "This is a crazy place," Wysocki observes.

Detota, 84, has been playing fiddle for 60 years by ear. ("And right now his ear hurts," Kalanoski quips.) He'd never been in a band until he started coming here. "I couldn't make a living, I'd starve to death, so I play for nothing," the Little Italy resident says in an accent that makes him sound like he's fresh in from the old country. "You live longer."

The band takes a break. In the silence, all attention falls on Stankowski as he puts a video in the barroom TV. It shows him and some friends rockfishing with balls of dough at 5:30 a.m. down at the Chester Street pier a few weeks back—proof, supposedly, that there's still good fishing to be had on the Baltimore waterfront. But the band's break is quick; the comical video comes off and the oompah sounds take over. Gino Wysocki lets out a cry: "The boss has got his harmonica!"

Stankowski pulls out a microphone he keeps behind the bar, and in between the concertina and the accordion floats the softer sound of Lucky's harmonica, playing "Green, Green Grass of Home."

Charles Cohen
November 17, 1999

Tall Tale

Seventy years ago, Baltimore's skyline gained a dash of soaring panache when our first true skyscraper—and for 44 years, our tallest building—reared its copper-and-gold roof over downtown. In December 1929, the Baltimore Trust Company moved into the 34-story, $6.6 million brick-and-limestone office tower the firm had erected on Light Street downtown, between Baltimore and Redwood streets. "It is a veritable temple of finance," promotional materials gushed at the time. "Its rugged outlines towering against the sky stands as an evidence of faith in a great city."

Talk about lousy timing. The stock market had just tanked, and the nation was tilting headlong into the Great Depression—

not the ideal moment for a bank to be cutting the ribbon on an expensive architectural edifice. Intended as a mammoth monument to Baltimore Trust's fiscal strength, the tower spent most of its first decade as a mammoth, money-losing white elephant. The company went belly up just two years after moving into its lofty, luxurious home, and by 1933 the building was half vacant.

Today, the behemoth is the Bank of America Building, the sixth name it's had over the years. (In the 1940s, it was, somewhat ignobly, called the O'Sullivan Rubber Company Building.) During World War II, when an alphabet soup of defense-related federal agencies occupied the building, cabbies took to calling the place "Little Washington." By any name, this looming legacy of a failed bank remains the most recognizable and handsome component of the downtown cityscape. Its upper floors are dramatically illuminated at night, and the mansard roof glistens with fresh gold leaf.

I recently sidled through the building's arched entranceway to see how this hunk of 1920s exuberance is doing on its 70th birthday. My guide is Michael Eckhardt, the building's affable property manager, who has consummate respect for the architectural grande dame under his care. While much of the building is big and showy, its many curious little details dazzle, too. Ornate bronze window grates are decorated with crabs, and carvings around the exterior doors depict epic Baltimore events such as the Great Fire of 1904 and the penning of "The Star-Spangled Banner." The 200-foot-long bank lobby—once billed as "one of the largest undivided banking rooms in the world"—sports a sumptuous mosaic floor and huge murals depicting three centuries of Maryland and Baltimore history.

We work our way skyward, pausing at various floors to ramble across the roofs of the tower's various setbacks and examine the gargoyle-like limestone carvings that festoon the building. There are giant bird and lion heads and smaller, Mayan-inspired human faces protruding from the tower's brick flanks. Architects call it an art deco building, but it's a conservative example of the genre. (It certainly doesn't have the deco drama of Manhattan's shimmering Chrysler Building, erected around the same time.) The various arched windows and buttresses give it an almost Gothic feel.

At the tower's inception, the entire 20th floor was given over to the swanky members-only Chesapeake Club, an array of dining, smoking, and lounging rooms rife with wood paneling and easy chairs. Today, the floor is a sea of beige cubicles. (Offices first invaded the club in the '40s.) Gone too is the 34th floor's Tower Service Club, a sort of sky-high men's spa where movers and shakers could get a shave, Turkish bath, massage, or workout (or bed down for a catnap) while their suits were pressed to perfection. The space where businessmen once luxuriated is now a drab, disheveled workspace leased by Bell Atlantic to maintain its rooftop equipment.

We've reached the top floor, but we go higher still. A stairway leads us into the interior of the oxidized-copper mansard roof, a windowless expanse brimming with pipes, wires, and ducts. (There's even an old pigeon house—a vestige, perhaps, of a pre-fax communication system.) I remark that it feels more like a basement. "It won't feel that way for long," Eckhardt says.

The final assault on the building's pinnacle involves a gulp-inducing series of lengthy iron ladders. And then we are 509 feet above downtown Baltimore, surveying the city from a 15-by-30-foot platform at the tower's crown. WBAL-TV's "sky cam" is in one corner, and a steel antenna rises from the center of the platform. (Local TV stations broadcast from here before the TV Hill antenna was built.) Earlier this year, a Johns Hopkins architectural student who wrote a paper on the building proposed to his girlfriend on this lofty perch, and it's easy to see why: It is a dizzyingly impressive spot. The city roars beneath us, and we can see as far as Towson to the north.

Turning to the south, the view is interrupted by the boxy,

squat-roofed Legg-Mason Building (erected in 1973 as the USF&G Building) a few blocks away. It now holds the title of Baltimore's tallest tower, beating out the Bank of America Building by 20 feet. But to my mind, it loses the beauty contest by a mile.

Brennen Jensen
December 15, 1999

Charmed Things

Battling Monuments

Sometime next year Baltimore will dedicate a public memorial to Frederick Douglass, the famed abolitionist who lived here in the 1820s and '30s prior to his escape from slavery. The memorial, to include a statue and an educational center, will be developed by the Living Classrooms Foundation at the west end of Thames Street in Fells Point, midway between two places Douglass lived as a child.

Douglass might be the most historically significant person ever to reside in Baltimore. Why then has it taken so long to give him this kind of recognition? Granted, there's already one statue of Douglass in town—but it's on the campus of Morgan State University, out of the general public's view.

I used to suppose that Baltimore's neglect of Douglass was due to civic embarrassment that this American hero lived here as a slave. More likely it is due to Douglass' legacy as a brilliant propagandist who helped win the Civil War by popularizing it as a crusade for emancipation. In this age of African-American ascendancy in the city's civic and cultural life, it's easy to forget that Baltimore in 1861 was heavily pro-secession and pro-slavery, and that Southern sympathies and official racism lingered well into the 20th century.

Our public statues stand as explicit reminders of this legacy. When the Douglass figure is installed next year, it will join at least four monuments honoring people who opposed his cause. The oldest is the statue of Roger Brooke Taney, which faces the Washington Monument in Mount Vernon.

A native Marylander, Taney was chief justice of the U.S. Supreme Court from 1836 to 1864. In 1857 he authored the infamous Dred Scott decision, ruling that slaves could not win freedom by escaping to a free state and that no black person could be a U.S. citizen. The statue was set up in 1887, long after the war that rendered Taney's decision—if not his sentiments—moot.

Two very different statues honor the Rebel military. The Confederate Soldiers and Sailors Monument, on Mount Royal Avenue near Mosher Street, drips with late-Victorian melodrama. Dating from 1903, it features a wounded soldier upheld by a laurel-bearing angel. Latin inscriptions include GLORIA VICTIS ("Glory to the vanquished") and DEO VINDICE, traditionally translated as "God is our defender."

Better known is the Lee and Jackson statue on Art Museum Drive. Reputed to be the only double equestrian statue in the United States, it represents the parting of generals Robert E. Lee and Thomas "Stonewall" Jackson on the eve of the battle of Chancellorsville. A friend of mine remembers admiring the monument from a child's perspective; she then believed that "purpose" and "so great"—the last and first words of the inscription wrapping around the pedestal—were the names of the two huge horses. As to the riders, there's a quotation from J. Henry Ferguson, who funded the memorial: THEY WERE GREAT GENERALS AND CHRISTIAN SOLDIERS AND WAGED WAR LIKE GENTLEMEN. Students of the Civil War might argue with that, but the statue went up in 1948, when America felt good about warriors.

Finally there's the monument to the Confederate Women of Maryland, at the corner of North Charles Street and University Parkway. Despite its title, this memorial almost transcends North-South partisanship, as it is a tribute to the good deeds of noncombatants. There are two female figures, one comforting a wounded soldier still clutching a battle flag. The rear of the pedestal reads, IN DIFFICULTY AND DANGER, REGARDLESS OF SELF, THEY FED THE HUNGRY, CLOTHED THE NEEDY, NURSED THE WOUNDED AND COMFORTED THE DYING.

Outnumbered by all of these Confederates, the city's sole Union statue stands at Charles and 29th streets. Dedicated in 1909 (and originally located in Druid Hill Park), the state-funded Union Soldiers and Sailors Monument might have been designed to trump its Confederate counterpart on Mount Royal Avenue: Unlike the Reb, the Yank is still marching, protected by not one but two allegorical figures. The placement of Lee and Jackson, across Wyman Park Dell from the Union monument, also seems strategic: Having flanked the Yank, they ride north while he still glowers southward. When at long last Frederick Douglass arrives, he'll help even the score—as he did 135 years ago.

Tom Chalkley
March 11, 1998

Candy Land

The passage of years erodes most old-timey, sugarcoated customs, but Baltimoreans' allegiance to their homegrown candy has persisted into mass-market modernity. Forget Godiva and the like—names such as Wockenfuss, Naron, Louis J. Rheb, and Log Cabin might as well be engraved on local family crests for the part they play in people's memories.

Evidence of that is especially apparent this time of year, when customers queue up as early as 6 a.m. at the Rheb factory on Wilkens Avenue in Southwest Baltimore to get their Easter chocolate.

"They sell out the place and then they shut the door," says Edward Malan as he stands in line—he's seen it happen.

Chocolate-making in Baltimore is not only neighborhood-based—it is intertwined with the classic immigrant story of creating a business out of family traditions.

"When the holidays came they would have their copper kettle and utensils in the basement that they used to make their

candies," says Jim Ross, founder of Naron Candy Company in Hampden. "Those that had a product that caught on, they would give up their day jobs."

The number of local candy makers has dwindled from about two dozen in the 1950s to a surviving handful, but those remaining have a place so long as Baltimoreans maintain a sweet tooth. "People eat candy no matter," says Bernard Rudell, owner of Log Cabin Candies, "even during the Depression."

In the 1930s Rudell was a jeweler and watchmaker who earned extra money making chocolate bunnies at home and selling them to Log Cabin Candies. The relationship worked out well for Rudell: In the late 1940s he bought the candy company, then located in the city on Charles Street. The Rudells set up shop in a tiny basement space in the Loch Ridge Shopping Center off of Loch Raven Boulevard. Bernard Rudell did watch repairs while selling bread, Breyer's ice cream, cigarettes, and his wife Edna's homemade chocolates.

"People would come for miles to get Breyer's ice cream," Edna remembers. "Now you can get it in any grocery store, but back then that brought a lot of customers and they tried our candies and they liked them."

By the late '50s Edna-brand chocolates had built up such a following that Rudell was able to buy property in Harford County, setting up shop in Fallston. Today Log Cabin specializes in making chocolates for fund-raisers, but during the Easter season the company get swamped by shoppers sorting through a menagerie of chocolate animals ranging from bunnies to bulldogs.

The Rheb Candy Company had similar beginnings. Louis Rheb started making candy in 1917 in the basement of one of the two Wilkens Avenue rowhouses that today serve as the company's factory, according to his daughter Esther. He began with jellies, moved on to brittles and toffees, then perfected the chocolate blend that gives Rheb candies their signature taste.

Even in the summertime, typically an off-season for candy,

"people are waiting for us to open the door," Esther Harger says.

After World War II a new kind of candy maker arrived on the scene. Jim Ross had compiled his recipes from a Parisian chocolatier Ross met while serving overseas in the Air Force. In 1946 the erstwhile airman joined with Gerald Naron to form the Naron Candy Company.

While most local sweets purveyors sold their products out of their own storefront, Naron sold candy wholesale for larger customers—gourmet shops, department stores—which in turn marketed it as custom-made. Starting out with Ross, Naron, their wives, and two employees, the firm has grown into a 65-person operation. Last year it merged with Mary Sue, another local candy maker.

While candy is as close as the nearest supermarket, Baltimoreans still go out of their way to stand in line at local candy makers. At Rheb's stall in Lexington Market, Buzz Chalk—wearing a T-shirt with the message GIVE ME ALL YOUR CHOCOLATE AND NO ONE GETS HURT—and his wife Pat are buying 17 pounds of candy for their neighbors in Wyman Park and for Buzz's American Legion buddies. Later Chalk will come downtown again to buy more chocolate as part of a Baltimore care package (including Rheb's candies, Utz potato chips, and Tastykakes) for his brother, who lives in Alaska. Chalk says his brother lives for these periodic tastes of home: "That's all he wants."

Charles Cohen
April 8, 1998

I Scream, You Scream

We all scream for ice cream. And the fact that there's a plethora of folks that hear us—be it Baskin-Robbins, Breyer's, or Ben & Jerry's—is due in large part to a Baltimorean named Jacob Fussell. Nearly a century and a half ago this erstwhile milk merchant fathered the ice cream industry. Fussell didn't invent ice cream; humanity has been enjoying some form of this sweet eat since ancient times. (Emperor Nero poured honey over scoops of snow special runners delivered to Rome from the peaks of the Apennines; Marco Polo brought back sherbet recipes from the East.) Fussell wasn't even the first to make ice cream in Maryland. (We know that Gov. William Bladen bellied up to a bowl of strawberry ice cream in 1700, and Baltimore newspapers were running ice cream ads as early as 1798.) But Fussell was the first in the nation to produce and peddle ice cream on a large scale. He was the Henry Ford of frozen desserts.

Fussell began his career by selling dairy products Pennsylvania farmers sent him via the Northern Central Railroad. It proved to be an erratic business. The cows were steady suppliers, but Baltimoreans were not always regular buyers. And in 1851, the story goes, Fussell found himself with an excess supply of cream. Rather than see it sour, he decided to make it all into ice cream, unloading it at the rock-bottom price of 25 cents a quart—less than half of what other ice cream makers charged. A hot and hungry populace eagerly scooped up his product, and Fussell found a new calling.

Following the twin principles of big batches and cheap prices, he went into the ice cream biz full time—and with sweet success. By 1856 he had opened manufacturing operations and parlors in Washington and Boston. Ice cream went from being a pricey confection for a few to a regular treat for many. (And there's more to commend Fussell for than ice cream entrepreneurship. A practicing Quaker, he was staunchly opposed to slavery. He worked on the Underground Railroad, and his outspoken abolitionism got him besieged by one of Baltimore's infamous angry mobs.)

Don't look for Fussell's name in your grocer's freezer—a larger firm bought the Fussell company in the 1920s and the founder's name was dropped. But in 1951 the local ice cream giant was given a gala centennial celebration. Thousands gathered around the East Baltimore intersection of Hillen and Exeter streets—site of Fussell's original operation—to dedicate a bronze plaque deeming the block the BIRTHPLACE OF THE ICE CREAM INDUSTRY. Politicos spoke, bands played, kids downed gallons of free ice cream, and Hollywood heartthrobs Tony Curtis and Piper Laurie were crowned the "Sweethearts of the Ice Cream Industry."

Helping to organize the festivities was another local ice cream icon: L. Manuel Hendler. His name too is gone from supermarket shelves, but it's probably not forgotten. Generations of Baltimoreans grew up eating Hendler's ice cream, which was sold from 1905 through the late 1960s. Indeed, Hendler's—billed as "The Velvet Kind"—was so ubiquitous in its day that many soda-fountain customers probably never knew other brands existed.

Hendler's big sales jump occurred in 1912, when he established a state-of-the-art ice cream factory on East Baltimore Street. There the chilly confection flowed forth without ever being touched by human hands (a far cry from Fussell's pre-refrigeration plant, with its manually cranked machines and mountains of ice).

Hendler's company dealt mainly in the big three—vanilla, chocolate, and strawberry—but the public also developed a hankering for the exotic. Hendler's ice cream scientists created dozens of curious flavors, including ginger for the Hutzler's tearoom and a unique tomato sherbet for the Southern Hotel (where it was served as a side dish rather than a dessert). The company's rum-soaked eggnog ice cream was a big seller around the holidays.

Ice cream was very good to Hendler, who lived in a white Reservoir Hill mansion local wags took to calling "Vanilla on the Lake." But like Fussell's before it, his company was eventually absorbed by a larger, national brand. The only places the Hendler name can be seen these days are antique shops, where the company's ice cream paraphernalia can occasionally be found.

Americans still eat a prodigious amount of ice cream. (According to the Washington-based International Ice Cream Association, the Baltimore metro area consumed 6.3 million gallons of it in 1996—enough to rank it among the top 10 ice cream-consuming cities in the United States.) So the next time you get an ice cream jones, raise a cone to Jacob Fussell and L. Manuel Hendler, vanished captains of a once-flourishing, soft and sweet city industry. As the poet Wallace Stevens wrote, "The only emperor is the emperor of ice cream."

Brennen Jensen
April 29, 1998

Walls of Fame

These days Robert "Dr. Bob" Hieronimus is probably best known as the host of *21st-Century Radio* on WCBM (680 AM)—a sort of New Age gadfly whose interests range from UFOs and astrology to environmentalism and rock 'n' roll. But long before he took to the airwaves, Hieronimus gained local fame as the creator of colorful, cryptic murals, some of which have become Baltimore landmarks. As 1998 marks the 30th anniversary of Hieronimus' mural-painting career, the time seems right for a tour of his extant work.

We begin at Levering Hall on Johns Hopkins University's Homewood campus. Upstairs, in the Office of Volunteer Services, behold "The Apocalypse," a 2,700-square-foot acrylic mural commissioned in 1968 by JHU's legendary activist/chaplain Chester Wickwire. "The Apocalypse" mixes politics with biblical prophecy: Miss Liberty sinks into the waves, an eagle is infected with corporate logos, a serpent spits fire. The style is often described as "psychedelic," but Hieronimus maintains that everything about the work is soberly symbolic. The dense mingling of ancient and modern icons sets the pattern for the murals that followed.

Next, chronologically, comes "America's Bicentennial, 1776-1976," painted in 1974 at Lafayette and St. Paul streets. The imagery here is less threatening than in the JHU mural, and slightly less cryptic: An allegorical figure of Columbia leans into a bald eagle; the Beatles' yellow submarine (a recurring Hieronimus image) is moored to Baltimore's Battle Monument. Surveying the scene is the eye-on-pyramid symbol familiar from the U.S. dollar bill, a motif that is virtually the artist's logo. The original palette was bold blue, green, red, and gold; these have faded over time to gentle pastels.

In the heart of Hampden, the "Congressional Medal of Honor" mural (1975) overlooks the corner of 36th Street and Roland Avenue. An eagle dangles banners bearing the names of two Hampdenites who earned the Medal of Honor in World War I. Hieronimus recalls this as a difficult assignment due to community restrictions and "the worst-condition wall I ever painted on." Ironically, it might be his most publicly visible painting.

The least-visible Hieronimus mural covers one side of an 18-inch-wide keyhole alley at 838 Tyson Street. This privately commissioned painting is a mystical celebration of Elisha Tyson, the abolitionist hero and city father for whom the street is named. Not content with mere history, Hieronimus worked in a unicorn, the Greek god Pan, and the by-then-obligatory yellow sub and pyramid. From the street you have to peer through a steel grate to get a glimpse.

In his 1976 "War Memorial" mural, Hieronimus continued in a historical vein with scenes of Baltimore's harbor in 1752, 1838, and 1857. In the foreground are several Lords Baltimore and, incongruously, George Washington crossing the Delaware. In the pastel harbor floats the early submarine *Argonaut*, and a certain other sub. As a pastiche of fact and fantasy, the mural is a good match for the eclectic deco/Roman style of the Memorial itself.

Crossing the harbor to the South Baltimore peninsula, we come to the "All-American City" mural (1977) at Fort Avenue and Lawrence Street, originally conceived as a sort of gateway to the Locust Point area. Immigrants, many of whom arrived via Locust Point, dominate the foreground; the 1977 city skyline spreads across the top. Unfortunately this huge image is now obscured by a Blockbuster video store, and two decades of sunlight have reduced its original pastel colors to near-subliminal tones.

Next-to-last stop: Lexington Market. Enter the Market East building at Eutaw and Lexington streets, hang a right, proceed to the counters of Muhly's Bakery and Park's Fried Chicken, and look up at "E Pluribus Unum," completed in 1986. This might be Hieronimus' masterpiece, incorporating all of his favorite themes, icons, and color codes, plus portraits of more than 30 people ranging from Ralph Waldo Emerson to burlesque queen Blaze Starr. It was also the last public mural for which Hieronimus strained his back muscles: He is now essentially retired from mural making, although he still gets involved when recruited. "A Little Help from Our Friends" (1996) at 3333 Greenmount Avenue was designed and largely funded by Hieronimus but executed by painters Katie Butler, Lyle Kissack, and Gerald Ross. It shows Gandhi, Martin Luther King Jr., Bob Marley, Bob Dylan, and others who, like Hieronimus, started out as radicals and became institutions.

Tom Chalkley
May 13, 1998

Whiskey Rebellion

*W*hiskey has been called "the water of life." That would seem to make Maryland dead and dry.

Time was, only four other states made more liquor than ours. In 1958, for example, Maryland distilleries poured out nearly 11 million gallons of booze, nearly half of it whiskey. In 1997, we produced nary a drop. Our cup runneth empty. We've no distilleries left.

But more was lost than just a once-flourishing industry. Maryland's chief potent potable was straight rye whiskey, a fiery amber liquid made around Baltimore and celebrated around the world. What Kentucky is to bourbon, what Russia is to vodka, so Maryland was to rye. And the bottles bore brand names reflecting their birthplace: Baltimore County, Owings Mills, Maryland Club, Maryland Pride, Toast of Maryland. (There was also a host of less geographically named Baltimore brands, such as Hunter, Old Horsey, and Happy Days.)

Don't look for those labels anymore. Out at Wells Discount Liquors, the voluminous liquor emporium on York Road at the Baltimore County line, the few ryes in stock are relegated to a dusty lower shelf. There are Jim Beam and Wild Turkey ryes, and one called Old Overholt. As it turns out, "old" is the key word when it comes to rye.

"The only people I sell rye whiskey to were born before World War II," store owner Mike Hyatt says. He pauses. "Maybe even World War I."

Among his "brown liquors," Hyatt says, rye is the slowest seller, though it does enjoy a slight seasonal sales spike: "At Christmastime a lot of old family recipes for eggnog call specifically for rye whiskey."

Only one storied local rye brand remains: Pikesville. Named after the Baltimore County community, it's now a product of Bardstown, Kentucky (though it was distilled, the label reports, "under an old Maryland formula"). Pikesville was last made in Maryland more than 25 years ago, a product of Arbutus-based Majestic Distilling Company, which today only bottles liquor made by other distilleries.

"It used to be a monstrous business. Now it's kind of a yesteryear thing," Majestic's president, Lee Schuman, says. "There were a lot a of people who swore that's what kept them alive—a shot of rye right before you go to bed cures what ails you."

Evidently, not enough folks have been taking their cure. Rye fans are a vanishing breed.

"Rye drinkers are generally older gentleman," Schuman explains. "When one passes away you lose a rye customer."

Oddly enough, you could say Richard Nixon is to blame for the death of Maryland-made Pikesville rye. In the early '70s, the president OKed grain shipments to the Soviet Union. Schuman says this sent grain prices through the roof.

"When you make rye whiskey, it has to age in a barrel a minimum of 36 months," he says. "Your money is tied up for three years. As a small, family-owned company, it wasn't cost-effective for us to manufacture rye whiskey."

Of course, Tricky Dick can't be solely blamed for the demise of Maryland rye. Changing customer preference is the real culprit. Drinkers developed a taste for less taste. Rye rose here in the first place, most accounts have it, with the growth of the German settlement in the mid-Atlantic. The immigrants grew rye, the kind of bread they enjoyed back in the old country. But just as rye bread is more pungent than white bread, so rye whiskey is more pungent than whiskeys made from corn or other grains.

"It's very flavorful—let's just put it that way," Schuman says in describing rye's kick. (H.L. Mencken wrote of his father's habit of ducking into the dining room for a shot of rye: "When he emerged he was always sucking a great whiff of air to cool off his tonsils.")

Maryland rye's high point came in the late 1930s, when some 15 million gallons of the stuff were aging away in warehouses from Cockeysville to Dundalk. But after World War II, people's palettes began shifting toward the lighter liquors— vodka, gin, rum—and sweeter, smoother bourbon. This less-taste trend was not unlike the one that did in local brewing (when Baltimore's numerous, tasty beers were bludgeoned under by anemic Budweiser and close-to-water Coors Light).

Of course, many things old are new again. Who would have thought such a vile pursuit as cigar smoking would come back? Local brewing is rebounding (albeit on a smaller scale), and small-batch whiskeys are now trendy.

"Some smart person with a great deal of money might be

able to reintroduce rye," Schuman says. "It's an acquired taste, but if people like single-malt Scotches, they could certainly enjoy a straight rye whiskey."

Brennen Jensen
May 27, 1998

Dial Tome

Want proof that Baltimore is the center of civilization? Go to the rose garden in Druid Hill Park.

Standing there in the middle of the garden is a sundial—and not just any sundial. This one tells time for more than a dozen places around the world, including the equator and the poles. It has a tantalizing mystery, too.

It looks like a giant piece of rock candy bronzed and augmented with 15 fins—one for each place for which it tells time. At belt-buckle level is Baltimore, marked at 0 degrees longitude. Of course, any geographer—or a geographically challenged writer with an atlas in his lap—will tell you that Baltimore's longitude is 76.38 degrees north. And regardless of what anyone around here tries to tell you, the rest of the world is not calibrated in relation to Baltimore.

The dial's oddities captivate George McDowell, an attorney whose fascination with the timepiece boarders on obsession. A past vice president of the North American Sundial Society, McDowell keeps tabs on the city's dozen public dials, from the stone-carved piece in Moreland Memorial Park Cemetery to the neglected rare dial in front of Johns Hopkins Hospital. He has pictures of them hanging in his living room. The Druid Hill sundial is McDowell's favorite. Give him a chance and he'll tell you about his amazement at how the designer configured the time settings without a model to go on and without using clocks. He'll also explain how the dial works on solar time, measuring how long it takes the Earth to rotate, which puts it out of sync with standard time, except (for reasons it would take several paragraphs to explain) at noon on December 12.

But what really has a hold on McDowell are the mysteries that swirl around the Druid Hill dial: The fact that the real designer's identity is not known, and that no one knows for certain where the dial was first installed.

McDowell discovered the sundial in 1992 when a friend who knew of his interest in the old-fashioned timepieces took him to the park and asked him how it worked. McDowell noticed the sundial was pointed in the wrong direction (it was 180 degrees off), most of the plates were damaged, and some of the gnomons—the vertical pieces that cast the shadows to tell time—were either missing or damaged. He fell in love. Before long he discovered that the multifaceted dial, called a "compendium dial," is one of only a few in the United States, and he started searching for the creator's identity and the date of installation.

The one clue was the dial's inscription: THIS DIAL WAS PRESENTED TO DRUID HILL PARK BY PETER HAMILTON, ESQ. IN 1892. REPAIRED AND RESET BY THE BOARD OF PARK COMR'S IN 1904.

"I've searched the city archives, the Maryland Historical Society, the Pratt library, the Smithsonian [Institution]," he says. "I think I have a copy of every place it was mentioned, every picture, every article."

A 1927 newspaper photo identifies Hamilton as the dial's maker, but a series of 1913 letters McDowell found in his research raise another possibility. Correspondence between Baltimorean Claude L. Woolley and George C. Maynard, curator of the Smithsonian Institution's Division of Mechanical Technology, was prompted by Maynard's inquiries about whether the dial was exhibited at the Philadelphia centennial celebration of 1876. Woolley wrote that he had spoken to an old builder named McCoy who told him that a "Mr. Mann," a partner in a stone-cutting firm, had told McCoy some 30 years earlier that he made the dial. (Peter Hamilton, it turned out, co-owned a stonecutting firm with a George Mann.) Woolley's letter indicates that after the centennial the dial was offered to Baltimore City but the offer was rejected. It ended up in front of Mann's Bolton Hill home, where it reportedly stayed until it was given to the park in 1892. (Whether the Druid Hill dial was exhibited in Philadelphia isn't clear; McDowell says what was called the "Centennial Dial" wasn't the Druid Hill dial, but he doesn't rule out the possibility that the latter was also shown at the 1876 exhibition.)

By the time McDowell happened upon the dial a century later, it had been uprooted from its longtime roost outside of park headquarters and relocated via earth-mover to the rose garden, near the Conservatory—a trip McDowell suspects caused some of the damage to the plates and gnomons. In 1993 he got the city's permission to restore the dial and face it in the correct direction. He retained Larry Lewis, an Ellicott City metalsmith, to rebuild the missing parts and repair the damaged ones. The restored dial was rededicated the following year.

Even more so than the mystery of the dial maker's identity, McDowell is tantalized by the question of how the designer chose the 13 places (beside the equator and the poles) for which the dial tells time—Baltimore; Cape Cod; San Francisco; Sitka, Alaska; Honolulu; Pitcairn Island in the South Pacific; Jeddo (a former Western name for Tokyo); Calcutta; Jerusalem; London; Cape Town; Fernando Po (a Western African island now known as Bioko); and Rio de Janeiro. Were they picked because all are at sea level, or was there some other connection?

"I would go down there and study it and make drawings and try to figure out...what was the common thread between those cities," McDowell says, pulling on a Parliament cigarette and leaning against his car to contemplate the dial.

The dial gives a longitude for all of the locations; several are incorrect, most by less than a degree, although the location of Honolulu is a full 3 degrees off. (McDowell suspects the dial maker mistook another Hawaiian island for Honolulu. "If it were Hilo it'd be perfect," he says.) Perhaps everything's just a little distorted when the world revolves around Baltimore.

Charles Cohen
July 22, 1998

A Tree Grows in Mobtown

In Chicago, Al Capone left his mark in the form of bulletholes. In Baltimore, he left a beautiful Japanese cherry tree. The tree still stands outside Union Memorial Hospital on 33rd Street and Guilford Avenue, where the notorious gangster was treated in the late '30s for syphilis.

It was 1939 and the 40-year-old Capone had just served seven years in prison, most of it at Alcatraz, for tax evasion. In the final year of his incarceration, his health deteriorated rapidly due to the sexually transmitted disease, a product of his younger days, when he was perhaps less concerned with the underworld and more concerned with getting under the covers.

Capone was transferred to a federal prison in Lewisburg, Pennsylvania, from which he was given an "unconditional" release on November 16. No sooner had the mob boss gained his freedom than he was linked to the murder of Edward J. O'Hare a week previous.

O'Hare, president of Sportsman's Park racetrack in Chicago, had lined up witnesses to testify against Capone in the government's 1931 income-tax case against the gangster, according to *The Chicago Tribune*. Capone had learned of O'Hare's betrayal two years earlier, the *Tribune* reported, and

vowed vengeance.

"As in all Capone killings, the big boys are all out of town" to establish alibis, an official with the Chicago prosecutor's office told the Associated Press. "There's no longer any doubt about it being a Capone job."

With such intrigue brewing, banner headlines in *The Evening Sun* greeted "Scarface Al"'s arrival at Union Memorial Hospital (for treatment, one article reported, of "paresis-brain disease") right after his release from prison. The big play in the local paper testifies to the mobster's grip on the American imagination, considering that the other news of the day merely concerned Hitler's push into Europe and the United States' efforts to stay out of World War II.

Capone's stay at Union Memorial has become somewhat legendary at the hospital. Pete Kerzel, spokesperson for Helix Health (which owns Union Memorial), is thrilled to be the keeper of such a story. A history buff and former newspaperman,

Kerzel says he's been unable to track down the records on Capone's stay (even if he did, he'd be barred by confidentiality requirements from releasing them), but his research has confirmed that Capone did suffer from syphilis and, as a result, "his mental state was going."

Capone stayed in a guarded two-bedroom suite on the hospital's fourth floor. According to Kerzel, Capone came to Union Memorial after Johns Hopkins Hospital refused to treat such an infamous character. A contemporary news account stated that Capone's family tried to soothe nervous hospital officials' fear of violent reprisals against the patient: All Capone's enemies, the family said, were either incarcerated or dead.

During his two-month stay, Capone kept a low profile, granting no interviews. His brother John, a Philadelphia businessman with no known mob connections (other than his famous sibling), acted as his mouthpiece. But Capone made no secret of how impressed he was with the care that he received at Union Memorial, expressing his gratitude with the gift of a flowering Japanese cherry tree. Whatever else his proclivities, Capone apparently had an eye for horticulture; every spring, the tree bursts into an impressive floral display.

"I bet you hundreds of Baltimoreans have sat and admired this tree," Kerzel says, "but very few knew where it came from."

Capone checked out of Union Memorial on January 8, 1940, but he didn't check out of Baltimore, moving instead to the rented home on Pimlico Road that his family had occupied during his hospital stay. ("Capone Moves Into Mt. Washington," *The Evening Sun* blared.) His stay was brief and apparently uneventful; in March, he departed for Florida, where he lived out his days ensconced in a Palm Island palace. He died of a heart attack on January 25, 1947.

Charles Cohen
October 21, 1998

Our Oracle

Among the Teletubbies, Furbies, Beanie Babies, and other trendy toys that were furiously unwrapped this holiday season, no doubt some of the old reliables worked there way into the mix—perhaps a century-old novelty plaything that's either delightful or demonic, depending on whom you ask. At least a few kids, I'm sure, found Ouija boards waiting for them under the tree.

If it's been a while since you used a Ouija—the so-called "mystifying oracle"—recall that it's a small board (cardboard these days) emblazoned with letters, numbers, and the words YES, NO, and GOOD BYE. You rest your fingertips on the heart-shaped, three-legged pointer device (a planchette, in Ouija-speak) which then (hopefully, supposedly, maybe) moves about the board spelling out or otherwise answering questions asked of it—either as the result of involuntary, perhaps subconsciously driven movement of the hand or the purposeful, otherworldly efforts of spirits, ghosts, and other ethereal entities.

Christian writer Edmund Gruss, author of *The Ouija Board: A Doorway to the Occult,* called Ouija-ing a demonic activity that can lead to possession, insanity, suicide, and murder. The less doctrinaire probably view Ouija as a harmless, giggle-inducing component of an adolescent sleepover, a provider of answers to questions along the lines of "Does that cute girl in algebra class like me?" While much of Ouija is debatable and mysterious, what is known is that the "talking board" was invented by Marylanders and produced in Baltimore by the millions.

The Ouija saga begins on the Eastern Shore 108 years ago, when a Chestertown coffin maker with fondness for the spiritual built the first such board. He quickly sold the idea to neighbor Charles Kennard, who, with borrowed cash, opened the Kennard

Novelty Company on South Charles Street in 1890 (the same year he received a patent on the device). Kennard is usually credited with coining the term "Ouija." (One story has it that he simply asked the board to name itself, and O-U-I-J-A is what it spelled out.) But Kennard wasn't long in the board biz; by 1892 his shop foreman, William Fuld, had patented a modified version of the device, and in an almost couplike maneuver, he took over company operations, moving them to North Central Avenue. Teamed with this brother Isaac, William Fuld launched the Ouija Novelty Company and whipped up widespread enthusiasm for the mystic device. (He said the name Ouija was derived from combining the French and German word for "yes.") Others soon began making and marketing "talking boards" of their own, including Isaac Fuld, who was forced out of the family firm in 1901 (over questionable bookkeeping practices, by some reports); the Fulds were foes from then on, both claiming to be father of the Ouija.

Purportedly after seeking guidance from his own oracle, William Fuld built a modern, three-story Ouija factory at the corner of Harford Avenue and Federal Street. The oracle was right: The fear and uncertainty of World War I sent sales soaring, as folks turned to the boards for battlefield news about loved ones, both living and dead. Soon Fuld had to do battle himself, in court, after the IRS tried to classify Ouija as a "sporting good" (making it taxable) rather than a novelty, which was tax-exempt. In 1922 the case went to the U.S. Supreme Court, which threw it out, leaving the board's status, according to a *Sun* headline of the time, on the "List of Unsolved Mysteries." Between making the Ouijas and battling the competition, the IRS, and his brother, William Fuld managed to find time to serve in the House of Delegates, representing Maryland's 6th District.

Ouija sales began to slide as the '20s wore on. In February 1927, while Fuld was adjusting a flagpole on the roof of his factory, he slipped and fell to his death. (There are those who suggest he jumped.) His offspring continued board production, enjoying another sales spike during World War II. Ouija continued to be made in Baltimore until 1966, when the Fuld family sold rights to the board to Parker Brothers. With the big-gun toy maker's backing, Ouija sales soared the following year; the board even outsold the firm's flagship game, Monopoly. Now a division of Hasbro, Parker Brothers still sells Ouija, though with little fanfare. The bottom of each board, however, still carries William Fuld's name.

Befitting Ouija's spiritual nature, the Fuld's first factory is now a funeral home. The Harford Avenue facility, meanwhile, has been scrubbed up and turned into the Harford Commons senior-housing complex. On a recent visit to the complex, the residents I met were surprised to hear their home was once a Ouija-board factory (and that its owner plunged to his death out front). At first, no one reported experiencing any spooky happenings in the erstwhile oracle factory. But then a woman offered that she had seen an "angel" the last time she did laundry. Perhaps it was William Fuld, back to check production of the board he did not father, but did make famous.

Brennen Jensen
December 30, 1998

Signs of the Times

Lady Bird Johnson was right: Billboards are ugly. Back in the '60s, while her husband grappled with prickly civil-rights issues and Vietnam, the First Lady fought to beautify the nation's highways. She envisioned them lined with fewer billboards and more wildflowers, a desire that helped bring about the passage of the Highway Beautification Act in 1965.

Unfortunately this landmark legislation does nothing for city streets. Billboards blanket Baltimore—gaudy, obtrusive, oversized placards hawking everything from malt liquor to heroin-detox services to Don Rickles in concert. When Mayor Kurt Schmoke dubbed us "The City That Reads," he probably wasn't thinking about the looming visage of Billy Dee Williams reminding us that COLT 45 WORKS EVERY TIME.

Of course, billboards date back to well before Lady Bird and Billy Dee. Today most are machine-printed onto sheets that are slapped onto permanently mounted boards, a scheme that makes it easy to switch the ads. Back in the day, however, billboards and signs were hand-painted and longer-lasting. While these early advertisements might have offended the aesthetic sensibilities of their original viewers, today these peeling, fading vestiges help us see a city that was.

Take 812 Madison Avenue, a four-story brick building dating back to the 19th century. On its northern side, quite visible from busy Martin Luther King Jr. Boulevard, are the words NEELY and ENSOR, manufacturers of fine carriages. Faint letters on the south side of this apparently abandoned structure present a rundown of the company products: BROUGHAMS, VICTORIAS, CABRIOLETS, PITTSBURGH ROCKAWAYS, SURREYS, BUGGIES, TRAPS. On my last visit to this site, the building was being torn down. Ironically, on my quest for history, amid the jumble of fallen bricks I found the cardboard sleeve for an early cylinder phonograph record—an Edison Amberol record, circa 1910, to be exact.

Old-sign spotting in Baltimore is much like bird watching: You spend a lot of time straining your eyes and bending your neck. This is how I found the painted letters on a wall at 425 North Eutaw Street advertising a men's restaurant bar (with the words LADIES INVITED underneath). The establishment's name begins with an "H," but the rest is illegible. To walk south from here is to enter the city's former shopping, garment, and wholesaling districts—prime sign-spotting territory. Here you can see painted placards for TOTTLES 5¢ AND 10¢ STORE,

BALTIMORE BARGAIN HOUSE, APPLEFELD CLOTHING, BALTIMORE HANGER CO., and other ghosts from the past.

While fading paint is one obstacle to sign reading, subsequent real-estate development is another. The sign on the south side of the Hippodrome Theater is now obscured by the roof of a neighboring structure. You have to climb the stairs of the Abell Building across the street for an unmolested view of the words LOEW'S HIPPODROME POPULAR MATINEES 10¢.

Sometimes painted billboards are too beautiful to be true. A building near Hollins Market sports a crisply painted billboard for HENDLER'S ICE CREAM, THE VELVET KIND, which was Baltimore's homegrown favorite 40 years ago. But locals tell me the sign appeared long after the Hendler's brand vanished from the freezer case; it was painted to add authenticity to Barry Levinson's 1990 film *Avalon*, some of which was shot nearby.

Perhaps no ancient painted billboard is as well-positioned in contemporary Baltimore as the VOTE AGAINST PROHIBITION sign high above the corner of Shakespeare Street and Broadway in Fells Point. Throngs of eager pub-crawlers stream past this sign every weekend, heartily enjoying their freedom of inebriation. Which brings me to my favorite old-Baltimore billboard: the Natty Boh sign on the north side of 1207 North Charles Street (home to Thai Landing restaurant). Its upper half is obscured by a stucco-like wall covering. Only the words WHAT A BEER can be read (but I'm sure they're prefaced by OH BOY!). Mr. Boh, in a natty blue suit, is shown running toward a bottle of the once-beloved brew. David Donovan, Baltimore "breweriana" collector (and authority on all things Boh), tells me that judging from the bottle's design the sign dates from about 1953.

You can't always find an expert to help you decipher and date a billboard; the Pratt Library's collection of vintage city directories is the next-best thing. This is where I learned that the mysterious stag bar on Eutaw Street might have been Hanratty's Tavern, which operated there in the 1950s. This is also where I learned that Neely and Ensor moved operations to Mount Royal

Avenue in 1910, the same year they made another significant business change: Their directory listing read, "Neely and Ensor: Carriages, Automobiles, and Garage."

Brennen Jensen
February 10. 1999

The Classic Touch

This is a column about columns—specifically, the classical Greek columns that abound all over Baltimore, on all kinds of buildings. They are so much a part of our architectural environment that we scarcely notice them, much less pause and contemplate this style's survival through more than 2,500 years of shifting civilizations, technologies, and fashions. What else in

our daily culture can claim such a long pedigree? Not the English language, not the Catholic Church, not even the Roman alphabet. In architecture, the only thing older is the use of bricks.

Anyone who took Art History 101 knows that Greek columns come in three principal varieties, Doric, Ionic, and Corinthian, plus a few off-brands resembling the Big Three. They differ most obviously in the shapes, called capitals, that top their shafts: The Doric is capped with a cushion-like shape, the Ionic with a scroll-like object, and the Corinthian with a fancy capital that looks like an arrangement of ferns and kale. In ancient Greece (where the Doric order appeared first, around 600 B.C.), columns were typically "fluted," or grooved, along their shafts. The Romans, who adapted the Greek style for their temples and palaces, often did without the grooves.

After Rome's decline, the classical style fell into disuse for more than a millennium, only to be revived—and elaborated upon—by the architects of the Renaissance. The columns have been with us ever since, cropping up wherever Western civilization breaks ground.

Baltimore took shape in the late 18th and early 19th centuries, an era that saw a third wave of classic Greek and Roman building styles. In so-called Classical Revival buildings, hometown architects modeled their masterpieces on ancient precedents. The prime example is the Basilica of the Assumption at Cathedral and Mulberry streets, called "Baltimore's greatest work of architecture" by John Dorsey and *City Paper* contributing writer James D. Dilts, whose *Guide to Baltimore Architecture* I ransacked for this article. First built in 1805, the Basilica has a strong Roman feel, with a vast interior dome and, out front, 10 huge Ionic columns upholding a temple-style roof.

At the corner of Watson and Lloyd streets south of Corned Beef Row is an especially historic specimen of the Doric style. Designed in 1845 by the prolific Robert Cary Long Jr., the Lloyd Street Synagogue is the oldest synagogue in the city and the third oldest in the nation. Its facade is a devout imitation of a pagan

Greek temple, columns and all. (Ironically, Judaism is one of the few things older than Greek architecture—by some 1,500 years.)

The rather pompous Corinthian style can be seen at the Masonic Temple at Charles and 39th streets, and at the Evergreen Mansion just north of Loyola College.

My favorite Greek-column factoid relates to a Renaissance-style structure, the Clarence M. Mitchell Jr. Courthouse downtown. Its Calvert Street facade features a gallery of eight 31-foot Ionic columns. Courthouse tour guides assert that these are the largest monolithic columns in the world, each one carved from a single block of marble. There are bigger columns in the world, but they're all (if the factoid is a fact) built from "drums," or sections.

Any casual drive through town will yield classical columns (and crude knock-offs) in great number and variety. They pop up as free-floating components in a dozen eclectic styles, fabricated from stone, wood, cast iron, cement, you name it, adorning the porches of rowhouses and bungalows, manses and museums. The classical look used to be so popular with moneylenders that a late-'40s *New Yorker* cartoon shows a tourist among the Greek ruins, remarking, "What gets me is why they made all their buildings look like banks."

Seriously, though, why did we make our buildings like the Greeks? America grew up infatuated with what our boy Poe called "the glory that was Greece and the grandeur that was Rome." Classical architecture symbolized Roman might, but also Greek democracy. At any rate, a couple of Doric columns, though dry-rotted and in need of paint, still lend a bit of dignity, a reminder that one's humble rowhouse is nonetheless one's castle.

Tom Chalkley
February 17, 1999

Still Stoned

Those of us who drive or ride in downtown Baltimore are all too conscious of the pavement. Potholes, trolley tracks, and seemingly gratuitous bumps in the road shake our bones and rattle our axles. But lucky us: A century ago, commuters had to contend with what we commonly—and mistakenly—call cobblestones.

"Cobblestones are round stones created by nature and dug out of a stream," says Pierce Flanigan, president of P. Flanigan and Sons, one of the city's major pavement contractors. The proper term for Baltimore's old road surface is Belgian block. Flanigan's great-grandfather imported the cut-granite blocks by the schooner-load from Maine and New Hampshire.

At the end of the 19th century, according to Carleton Jones' *Streetwise Baltimore*, 75 percent of the city's streets were surfaced with stone. By Pierce Flanigan's estimate, some 70 percent of downtown Baltimore's asphalt streets were laid on top of the old granite surfaces. The cushioning layer of asphalt runs anywhere from 2 inches to 8 inches deep, he says; any deeper, and the road surface begins to overwhelm curbs and other infrastructure. "For the last 15 years we've been taking a milling machine and grinding off 2 inches of the existing pavement" when a road needs resurfacing, Flanigan says.

Sometimes an old road is so deteriorated that contractors do what he calls a "complete reconstruction project," tearing up the old pavement and starting again from the dirt up. Old Belgian block is salvaged for re-use wherever extra charm and traffic safety are called for. The foot of Broadway in Fells Point was recently repaved with recycled stone; up the street, at Johns Hopkins Hospital, the rumbling granite serves as what planners call a "traffic-calming device."

Yet there remain a few places where only the most cursory

efforts have been made to bury Baltimore's old streetscape. At the bottom end of Caroline Street, exposed blocks can be found in association with disused railroad tracks, possibly (Flanigan guesses) because the rights-of-way still belong to the railroads, not the city, and serious repairs could involve jurisdiction disputes.

More mysteriously, Central Avenue has been allowed to persist as a sort of pavement museum. Between Fayette and Monument streets, Belgian blocks, worn cobble-smooth by decades of horse and wagon traffic, well up through eroded patches of more recent, less durable stuff, in much the same way that rocks weather up through the soil. Trolley tracks run up and down Central. Just below Orleans Street, there's a set of rail switches where tracks branch off to the east and west. The tracks are lined with stones, the pavement pattern turning gracefully with the curves of the rails. Side by side with the stones, apart from the rails, lie lanes of old brick pavement, smoother than the blocks but perhaps too fragile to bear the brunt of trolley traffic. Concrete and various grades of blacktop lie in scabby puddles atop the orderly rows of bricks and blocks, a sort of found-sculpture essay on the theme of order vs. chaos. In some spots, the asphalt is worn down, thin as leather; in others, an inches-deep pothole offers a peek at the bright red brick below.

Central Avenue is a broad, moderately busy road in spite of its surface flaws. Is its lack of maintenance due to political disregard for the neighborhood's project-dwelling residents? Or did benign planners notice that the rugged road surface protects schoolchildren from speeding cars? (Two elementary schools and Dunbar High School lie along the rugged stretch of Central.)

Pierce Flanigan attributes the state of the street to an engineering problem that predates the granite: "There's a big 19th-century culvert under Central Avenue.... The discussion is about whether to do a complete reconstruction on the culvert, or to do just the street." It would be hard to redo the street, Flanigan says, without further damaging the ancient culvert, and opening up the culvert for repairs would mean significant disruption of east-west traffic.

Old maps show that the culvert contains what's left of a stream once known as Harford Run, which defined the boundary between Old Town and Fells Point. Long forgotten by Baltimoreans, the stream still makes its presence felt on the surface.

Tom Chalkley
March 10, 1999

Anchor Man

It's an old ship's anchor, and a big one. Forged of iron, it stands perhaps 8 feet high. A pair of hooklike arms curve outward and upward from the base, making the maritime icon about as traditional-looking an anchor as you'll ever see.

Except for the fact that it's painted metallic gold. Odder still, it sits propped up against St. Ann's Catholic Church in the hardscrabble neighborhood of East Baltimore/Barclay. There are no docks or ships in this inner-city locale. The harbor is a good mile away.

"Oh, it's the real thing," Sister Joanna Barasha, the church's pastoral administrator, assures me as I rap my knuckles against the weighty device (being careful not to step on the petunias and ivy swirling around its shadow). "Most people around here are used to seeing it."

There is a story surrounding it, of course. The anchor was here before the rowhouses that now engulf it. It was here before the 147-foot-high bell tower it rests against became part of the East Baltimore skyline. The anchor's tale begins long ago and far away—in the Gulf of Mexico in 1833, to be exact. It was one

of two anchors aboard the 179-ton brig *Wanderer*, commanded by Capt. William Kennedy, who had been a seaman since the tender age of 14. While off the coast of the Mexican port of Vera Cruz, a mighty gale bore down on Kennedy's craft as it lay at anchor near the tiny island of Sacrificios. Wind and waves battered his brig, and one of the anchors gave way. If the other anchor had failed, the ship would have been dashed against the rocky coast. The sailors aboard feared they were lost—all except Kennedy, who was alone in feeling hopeful. The story goes that while the deck pitched violently beneath him, he made a sacred vow that if the anchor held he would give up the seafaring life and build a church in honor of St. Ann, the patron saint of sailors.

The anchor didn't budge. The winds soon calmed. The *Wanderer* emerged worse for wear, but intact.

Kennedy piloted the plucky brig to Baltimore, where he

bade goodbye to the sea. Welcoming him home (to stay) was his wife of two years, the former Mary Ann Jenkins, daughter of a wealthy old Baltimore family. After working at his father-in-law's York Road tannery, Kennedy struck out on his own. He helped found the Mount Vernon Cotton Mills, a large factory along the Jones Falls that produced sail cloth and other woven goods. The erstwhile ship's captain became a captain of industry and ensconced himself in a rambling estate called Oak Hill just north of Green Mount Cemetery in what was then Baltimore County. (North Avenue—once also called Boundary Avenue—was the city limit from 1816 to 1888.) Kennedy, who'd retained his fateful anchor, placed it at Oak Hill's York Road entrance.

Perhaps it was his regular carriage rides past the icon that ultimately sparked him to fulfill the second part of his storm-induced pledge. He donated $50,000 toward erecting a church on a corner of Oak Hill's capacious grounds. Kennedy witnessed the laying of the St. Ann's cornerstone in the spring of 1873, but he died a mere six months later. The handsome Gothic-revival church, designed by the architecture firm Baldwin and Price, rose nonetheless. Kennedy and his wife (who also died in 1873) were ultimately buried in vaults beneath the church.

Meanwhile streets were cut through the environs (including an Oak Hill Avenue and a Kennedy Avenue), rowhouses were built, and the countryside turned into a city neighborhood. St. Ann's developed, too, adding both a school building and a convent. And after Oak Hill fell to the wrecking ball in the mid-1890s, its anchor was dragged over to decorate the churchyard.

As with many Baltimore neighborhoods, the community in the shadow of St. Ann's steeple was in decline by the 1960s. Middle-class residents, both white and black, began to vacate the area—leaving boarded-up buildings, crime, and grime in their wake. St. Ann's former school is now a homeless shelter, its convent a youth center. And the ancient anchor remains. A couple of times it was stolen and had to be rescued from the scrap yard (God only knows how anyone moved the hefty hunk of iron). Today it wears a fresh coat of gold spray paint, and amid rough seas of a different sort, the artifact from the long-gone *Wanderer* is a symbol of hope and strength; it is holding on anew.

Brennen Jensen
June 2, 1999

Out of Key

Try to imagine the chatter that would have ensued if the following folks had bumped elbows over a cocktail-party hors d'oeuvre table: Robert Kennedy, Mae West, the British Minister of Transportation, Fabian, the mayor of Jersey City, Milton Berle, and Dwight Eisenhower. Would West ask the Brit minister to peel her a grape? Would Fabian criticize Ike's financial support of France's continuing hegemony in Indochina?

Probably not. Most likely everyone would nosh in silence. Unless, of course, the subject of Baltimore came up. Here would be common ground for this diverse crew—all of whom, at one time or another, received the "key" to our city.

Presenting visiting dignitaries and celebrities with a ceremonial key to the city is a hoary gambit practiced by municipalities large and small. The custom may have its origins in feudal days and the age of walled towns: Legend has it that visitors who presented themselves at the locked town gate would be tossed a key if they were determined to be friendly (that is to say, not bent on rape and pillage).

It's not clear when Baltimore got into the key-to-the-city game. A 1907 postcard I scored at a flea market depicts such a key, and bears the words COME AND THE TOWN IS YOURS. The real focus of the card, however, is Old Home Week, a civic

celebration in which erstwhile Baltimoreans were invited back to see how the downtown was rebuilt in the wake of the 1904 fire.

Baltimore's first official key to the city might have rolled out in 1936. It was a curious token, an example of a "key on a key." The 13 1/2-inch long keys were carved out of an ancient wooden beam left over from renovations at the Flag House and bore pictures of the building and Francis Scott Key. A gross of such keys was delivered to Mayor Howard Jackson that year at a cost of $75. Eisenhower was sent one in 1945 following the Allied victory in Europe. The wooden souvenirs were handed out to notable visitors (Dale Carnegie and opera diva Eva De Luca, for example) until 1954, when Mayor Thomas D'Alessandro ushered in a new, gold-plated key. (The Flag House beam had long since been used up.) About 100 visitors a year left Baltimore with these shiny keys in their pockets.

Mayor Theodore McKeldin, who warmed the chair under City Hall's big desk from 1943 to '47 and 1963 to '67, was another prolific key-giver. In 1963 he deemed the gold key "cheap-looking" and unveiled another wooden model—one that, coincidentally, bore his name.

Here, alas, is where my key-to-the-city research grinds to a halt. (Maryland Comptroller William Donald Schaefer was presumably too busy wrestling with the state's finances to return calls seeking information on what, if any, ceremonial keys he dispensed during his 16 years as Charm City's chief executive.) One thing is certain: Baltimore doesn't have a key anymore.

"I can't recall when the last time there was a key to the city," says Clinton Coleman, spokesperson for Mayor Kurt Schmoke. "The mayor hands out bookmarks, and we use honorary citizenship instead of keys. It's a citation that proclaims you an honorary citizen of Baltimore." (Boris Yeltsin, Bishop Desmond Tutu, and some members of the Cuban national baseball team have walked off with this honorific.)

The old keys seem to be gone, too. (Thankfully, the Flag House Museum saved one of its wooden ones for posterity.) "We don't have a city key here," City Hall curator Jeanne Davis says. "We have a key to another city somewhere in a storeroom, but not a key to Baltimore."

Coleman says the city-key concept is more or less passé, but it's certainly not dead. Just ask the folks at Winchester, Indiana's Beachler Enterprises, a mom-and-pop company that makes nothing but engraved ceremonial city keys.

Beachler offers only one model, which sells for $10 (less when bought in quantity). "The key is of solid brass and weighs half a pound," company literature proclaims. "This is not an ordinary key, but is useful, as it is also a bottle opener."

"We ship about 600 to 700 keys a month," company secretary-treasurer Gary Gray says. He names Hazard, Kentucky, and Selma, Alabama, as two of Beachler's better customers.

Personally, I find something municipally ignoble about the key to one's city being used to pop the cap off a brewski. But then, who knows—notable visitors to Baltimore could soon be doing just that if the city key is reinstated. Coleman, whose boss leaves office in December, has this final word on the subject of a key to Baltimore: "Check with the next administration."

Brennen Jensen
August 4, 1999

Postscript: Mayor Martin O'Malley's administration has no plans to revive the key to the city.

Photo Credits

DAVID O. BARRANCO
Bromo Seltzer Tower photograph

JOHN ELLSBERRY
157

MICHELLE GIENOW
27, 47, 89, 102, 107, 113, 172

SAM HOLDEN
31, 44, 77, 100, 139, 165

JOSEPH KOHL
150

JEFFERSON JACKSON STEELE
55, 58, 61, 68, 92, 135, 141, 148, 178, 181

Column Credits

TOM CHALKLEY
Green Acres p. 25, Free Press p. 35, Excuse Her Dust p. 46, Fish Story p. 54, Lotus Land p. 74, Soul Sister p. 83, Bones but No Bonapartes p. 89, Small Town p. 97, Written in Stone p. 102, Top This p. 104, Old Alma Mater p. 107, Upward Mobility p. 112, The Birds p. 115, Mysterious Island p. 129, Battling Monuments p. 147, Walls Of Fame p. 155, The Classic Touch p. 172, Still Stoned p. 175

CHARLES COHEN
French Connection p. 3, Immigrant Song p. 8, A Dog's Life p. 17, On the Waterfront p. 19, Full of Beans p. 28, Oil and Water p. 31, Waxing Historic p. 41, Blow Up p. 43, The Courtroom Kidnapper p. 49, Holy Spirit p. 61, Old Money p. 71, Beautiful Swimmers p. 76, The Long Way Home p. 79, Aquatecture p. 99, Trains of Thought p. 117, Hog Heaven p. 126, Polka Parlor p. 137, Candy Land p. 150, Dial Tome p. 161, A Tree Grows in Mobtown p. 164

BRENNEN JENSEN
Blood Money p. 6, Song of Ourselves p. 11, Awl-Mighty Mobs p. 14, Mobtown Motors p. 22, Ms. Hi-De-Ho p. 52, For the Birds p. 57, The Odd Father p. 65, Sam the Joke Man p. 68, Far East Baltimore p. 91, Shop Talk p. 94, Bunny Trail p. 110, Armory Show p. 120, Royal Treatment p. 123, Lounge Acts p. 131, Tales From the Crypt p. 134, Tall Tale p. 141, I Scream, You Scream p. 153, Whiskey Rebellion p. 158, Our Oracle p. 167, Signs of the Times p. 169, Anchor Man p. 177, Out of Key p. 180

About the Authors and Editor

TOM CHALKLEY is a *City Paper* contributing writer and a freelance illustrator and cartoonist. He grew up in Kensington, Maryland, when it was a small town rather than a suburb. He attributes his taste for grotesque wonders of the past to being raised in a circa-1890s farmhouse, reading the 1911 World Book encyclopedia, and exploring Civil War battlefields as a child. He has been writing and drawing for *City Paper* since 1979, shortly after he moved to Baltimore from Washington, D.C., and realized he'd come home. He lives in the Beverly Hills neighborhood with his wife, Ruth Quinn, and their two daughters, and spends much of his spare time at the Enoch Pratt Free Library studying old maps.

CHARLES COHEN is a *City Paper* contributing writer and a freelance journalist, scavenging for stories others miss or leave behind and trying to make a living at it. He was born and bred in Baltimore and has been writing for local and national newspapers and magazines since graduating from the University of Maryland in 1985. Along with *City Paper*, he has written for *The Sun*, *Baltimore Magazine*, *The New York Times*, *The Christian Science Monitor*, *People*, and *Entertainment Weekly*. He lives in Fells Point with his wife, Amy Lynwander.

BRENNEN JENSEN is a *City Paper* staff writer. As a Baltimore buff, he is somewhat embarrassed to admit that he was born in Washington, D.C., and raised in Silver Spring, Maryland. Neither was his idea. College brought him to the Baltimore area in 1981, and since 1986 he has lived in a series of crumbling Charles Village rowhouses. He filed his first *City Paper* piece (about Baltimore, Ireland) in 1990 and joined the staff in 1996, covering planning, economic development, and neighborhood issues and reviewing the odd play along with his "Charmed Life" duties. When not pounding the pavement for *CP*, he collects old records and old radios, drinks Natty Boh, plays sloppy bass guitar, and earnestly attempts to ballroom dance.

ANDY MARKOWITZ is editor of *City Paper*, a position he has held since February 1996. Previously he worked as a reporter and editor for newspapers in the Washington suburbs and as a freelance writer and editor. He takes sole credit for having conceived the "Charmed Life" column after having an altogether dissimilar column suggested to him by a colleague and having totally unrelated ideas pitched to him by the authors of this book. His proudest professional achievement is having interviewed Monty Python's Terry Gilliam twice. He lives in Charles Village with his wife, Barbara Frye, and Tiny, the most beautiful cat in the world.

Charmed Books from Woodholme House

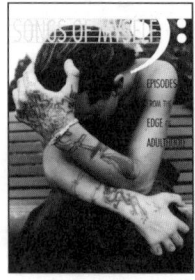

Diane Scharper (ed.) **SONGS OF MYSELF: EPISODES FROM THE EDGE OF ADULTHOOD** / 304 pp., $18.95
Finest essays from college memoir writing class. Scharper teaches at Towson University and reviews books for many newspapers, including *The Washington Post* and *The New York Times*. "No matter how intense or mild the tone is, each story reminds readers that one is never too young to experience tragedy, loss, love, and happiness."—*City Paper*

Carolyn Males, Carol Rolnick, Pam Goresh
WISH YOU WERE HERE! A GUIDE TO BALTIMORE CITY FOR NATIVES AND NEWCOMERS / 448 pp., $19.95
This guide sneaks a peek at what's unique about this storied port city—kitsch, culture, characters, and cuisine. Covers places to shop, eat, and stay with the best in Baltimore history and folklore. "The most comprehensive book on our town that I have ever seen. It's a great book."—Marc Steiner, WJHU

Eugene L. Meyer **MARYLAND LOST AND FOUND...AGAIN** / 288 pp., $15.95
Not for nothing has Maryland been called "America in Miniature." For to write about Maryland is to write about America. Meyer writes for *The Washington Post* and various magazines. "The book's strength lies in its interesting characters." — *Southern Living*

Rafael Alvarez **ORLO AND LEINI** / 192 pp., $14.95
Spun from the streets and alleys of Alvarez's "Holy Land"—a gritty, beautiful east Baltimore neighborhood—these stories transcend place to explore faith, love, and truth. Alvarez covers the city he loves for *The Sun*. "If Jimmy Breslin had grown up in Baltimore, he might have written stories like these."— Madison Smartt Bell

410.532.5018
info@woodholmehouse.com